An arc on a Zulu pot can represent ... to the great hut, that in turn represents the womb.

It isn't just the ancient language of shape and decoration, or the fascinating journey from traditional form to contemporary interpretation, or the thrill of discovering the magical connection between hand and mind; it's all these things and more that make us so proud of our longstanding support of South African craft and our association with this inspiring book.

Craft SA is not just a celebration of individual creativity, it's a privileged glimpse at the development and achievements of our craftspeople in South Africa. Every page informs the mind, intrigues the eye and delights the spirit.

Craft SA is the first book of its kind in South Africa.
A rite of passage? Perhaps.
A revelation of the talent around us? Definitely.

First National Bank
A division of FirstRand Bank Limited

Proudly South African since 1838
www.fnb.co.za

FCB JHB FMB19607

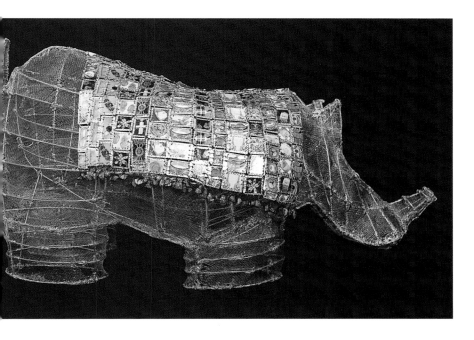

craft
south africa

craft
south africa

traditional | transitional | contemporary

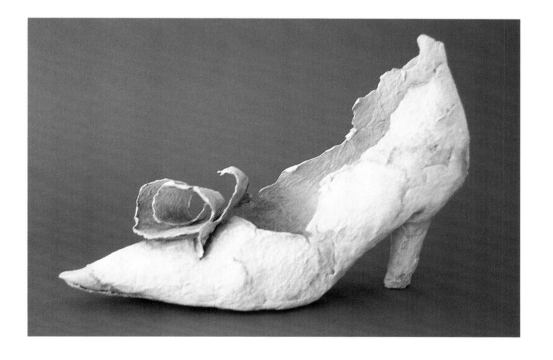

Susan Sellschop | Wendy Goldblatt | Doreen Hemp

First edition, first impression 2002
Published by Pan Macmillan SA (Pty) Ltd,
Hyde Park Corner, Hyde Park 2196 South Africa

ISBN 0 62029 227 X

Publisher: Dusanka Stojakovic, Pan Macmillan
Publishing Consultant: Louise Grantham, the-e-junction
Publishing Management: Zann Hoad, Sharp Sharp Media
Editor: Sean Fraser, PHRASEworks
Designer: Lore Watterson, DeskLink™ Media
Layout and Production: Sacha Traest, Kate Jackson & Chris Watterson, DeskLink™ Media
Printed and bound by Interpak Books, Pietermaritzburg
Paper: SAPPI HannoArt environmentally friendly paper supplied by Peters Papers.

Images on title pages:

Front cover: **Wola Nani**, bowl made from recycled paper labels formed over a mould.

Page 1: **Beverley Price**. Rhino – *Mapungubwe Re-mined*. Galvanised wire, aluminium, paint, laminated paper, pyrite (fool's gold).

Page 2: **Lobolile Ximba**. Doll. Fabric, beads, cardboard, shoes, wool, found objects, metal. Kim Sacks Gallery.

Page 3: **Verona Higgs**. Shoe. Hand made paper and acrylic paint.

Page 5: **Karosswerkers**. *Risaba Crossing*. Fabric and embroidery threads.

Page 6: **Ntombi Nala**. Ceramic vessel. Carved and burnished clay. Kim Sacks Gallery.

Contents Page and Opposite: Woman's scarf, back decoration or Mfengu. Textile, beads, buttons. (Collection: The Standard Bank Foundation of African Art, housed at The University of the Witwatersrand Art Galleries).

craft south africa

At the center of a nation's soul sits its cultural heritage. Craft marries so many strands. It brings together the strictly utilitarian and the decorative. It is wonderfully egalitarian because many of the basic skills are transmitted from one generation to another, to every member of a community. It assumes that we can all be creative. Yet every piece of craft bears the stamp of the individual.

South Africa is a society blessed with diversity, a diversity, which not only spans many cultures, but also one which spans age, gender, urban, rural. Ours is also a society where development and growth has sadly undermined or eroded some art forms yet also spawned new uses for new materials.

I find it quite exciting that so many new materials are increasingly being used to produce very traditional objects which are becoming very firmly identified as quintessentially South African. My favourites include the very colourful telephone wire baskets, the plastic chickens and the bowls made out of discarded canned pilchards labels. The Gertrude Posel Gallery in Johannesburg has an outstanding collection of traditional adornments like necklaces, anklets, belts and bridal skirts where modern items have been successfully recycled and comfortably placed next to traditional beadwork to produce truly unique objects which are works of art.

Exciting too is the way in which artists and crafts people are taking very universal art forms to new heights. Think what Jabu Nene and Ardmore are doing for global standards in ceramics and pottery. Think of the outstanding works of embroidery being produced by women in our far-flung rural areas. The tapestry in the Provincial legislature of Mpumalanga is increasingly being recognized as one of the most outstanding pieces of tapestry produced towards the turn of the century and deservedly so – it is just simply breathtaking. It does rather make my little African heart swell with pride when I notch up the many examples of how we South African are sitting at the center of enhancing universal art forms and contributing new exciting ones.

I feel our country is turning an important corner. I believe that we are beginning to walk more confidently into our future. Our steps are stronger, we are more confident to explore who or what we are as a modern, African nation. We can dream again, we can push the boundaries. We can assert with confidence that we are African and very sophisticated – the two are not mutually exclusive. Africa's time has come and we are proud to be at the cutting edge of it. Nowhere is this more apparent than in our outstanding crafts and the arts as whole.

I hope that you will enjoy as much as I did, the journey which the authors take us on through the book. It is a book which is long overdue. It is an initiative with which I am proud to be associated.

Enjoy!

Cheryl Carolus
C.E.O. South African Tourism

contents

craft in context

Craft objects have a universal attraction that crosses cultural and geographic borders and transcends time. The global interest in the traditions of other nations is supported by the worldwide desire to travel, as well as by programmes and articles in the media. A South African pottery bowl or an old Zulu milk pail can feasibly be found in a loft apartment in New York or a home in New England or, in fact, anywhere else on earth. The form, the volume and the integrity of the material introduce a connection to the roots of a living culture and bring a sense of the permanence of the creative spirit of mankind into the living space. Rebecca Matibe, working on the clay floor of her traditional homestead on the other side of the world in South Africa, may have made the pot and imbued it with her indigenous knowledge, skill and innate design ability, or the unknown maker of the milk pail may have carved it from a log of wood for his family to use, some generations ago.

In order to highlight the juxtaposition of the traditional and the contemporary, this book has been divided into three parts – Traditional, Transitional and Contemporary. The path of the ancient practices of making objects by hand using the materials available is followed through to the transitional changes in technique and material and finally to the creation of contemporary designer wares and one-of-a-kind craft

OPPOSITE PAGE:
Wall with baskets from all over Africa. Saxon Hotel.
Designed by **Stephen Falke**.

THIS PAGE, FROM TOP:
Basedi ba Bapedi. Thickly woven baskets from Limpopo; **Reuben Ndwandwe**. Open basket with a unique method of double weaving; **Linkie Wessels**. Large poplar baskets (Collection: Saxon Hotel)

objects. This is a fascinating tale of the intuitive creativity of craftspeople in a country of widely mixed and diverse peoples all contributing their own knowledge, skills and, frequently, their humour and whimsy to a pool of crafts that is unique to South Africa. We have also included examples of the way craft objects can be introduced into interior design and how they can be displayed to their greatest advantage.

We are frequently asked to define 'craft' and explain where it begins and ends and how it differs from 'art'. Perhaps it can be defined as useful and aesthetically pleasing objects created mainly by hand using specific materials and developed skills. Craftspeople generally begin the process of object making by choosing the material and the technique they will use, whereas an artist will begin with a concept and then choose the material to suit it. Craft objects can also veer towards design, with the designer deciding on the purpose of an object then choosing the appropriate material. In an African context, there is really no distinction between 'craft' and 'art'.

Bruce Metcalf the British ceramist, suggests that 'Craft-as-a-class-of-objects,

- must be an object – cannot be text alone or performance as art can.
- must be made substantially by hand, utilising the hand itself, hand tools and, to some degree, power tools.
- can be identified by the use of traditional craft materials, use of traditional techniques and addressing a traditional craft context.

These criteria are elastic – craft can retain one out of three and still be recognised as craft.'

In all these definitions, it is clear that crafts must be made predominantly by hand, and the skills and traditions are of prime importance.

THIS PAGE:
Beaded Ndebele bridal cape or *linaga*.
(Collection: Kim Sacks)

yesterday

In former times it would not have been unusual to find craftspeople making pots or bowls or wooden spoons in every community. They were needed for use in the household or for ceremonial or ritualistic purposes. Today it is still possible to find a basketmaker diligently preparing materials to be woven into a time-honoured form or a man sitting under a tree skilfully hollowing out the bowl of a long wooden spoon. Places of worship continue to use handmade chalices and candleholders, and very often the clothes and garments of the dignitaries are hand woven and embroidered according to age-old customs and rites. It is no longer vital to make these objects by hand, yet, craftspeople continue to make them and they continue to be used. Traditional, handmade objects are collected and conserved by museums and connoisseurs because their use and purpose throw light on past ways of life and the traditions of former cultures. They also play an important role in the popularisation of craft and its many traditions by holding curated exhibitions of the objects.

THIS PAGE, FROM TOP:

Siphiwe Nala. Ceramic pot with beer-pot cover or *imbenge;* Zulu beer-pot cover or *imbenge*. Beads and fibre. (Collection: Standard Bank Foundation of African Art, housed at the University of the Witwatersrand Art Galleries); Plastic-coated wire. (Collection: Standard Bank Foundation of African Art, housed at the University of the Witwatersrand Art Galleries)

the iron age and traditional arts and crafts

Thomas N Huffman

School of Geography, Archaeology and Environmental Studies, University of the Witwatersrand

Southern African arts and crafts have a long history, dating back to what archaeologists call the Iron Age. This history centres on Bantu-speaking people. Like others around the world, Bantu-speaking Iron Age societies were community orientated, emphasising the group over the individual. This communal perspective allowed for a continuity of traditional styles that are still in evidence today.

We know from historical linguistics that the Bantu language family evolved in the Nigeria/Cameroon border area of West Africa (Greenburg 1955). In about 1000BC, Western Bantu-speaking people moved into the Congo Basin as root-crop agriculturalists and oil-palm horticulturalists (Vansina 1984). Those who stayed in the homeland evolved Eastern Bantu and incorporated domestic grains, domestic animals and metal production into their way of life. At some point between 200BC and AD200 they left the

THIS PAGE:
Gold bowl (original). Mapungubwe. Burial item.
(Collection: SASOL African Heritage Exhibition housed at the University of Pretoria).

OPPOSITE PAGE, FROM LEFT:
Decorated terracotta pot. Mapungubwe; Large spouted pot. National heritage site. Mapungubwe (Collection: SASOL African Heritage Exhibition housed at the University of Pretoria).

homeland and moved east and south. Most of the Iron Age in southern Africa involves the archaeology of Eastern Bantu-speaking peoples.

From their homeland in West Africa, Eastern Bantu speakers brought with them a rich array of crafts. Many, however, were created from perishable materials, so what remains are usually those made from more durable substances such as clay, metal and glass.

Clay

As settled agriculturalists, Early Iron Age people needed pottery in a multiplicity of shapes and sizes. Indeed, the same variety of functional types that were in use in rural areas until relatively recently has been found in the earliest settlements. Ceramic assemblages from Broederstroom (Mason 1986) in the Magaliesberg and Gokomere (Huffman 1976) in Zimbabwe, for example, include large and small jars for holding liquids, bowls for cooking porridge and relishes, and other bowls for serving. Early ceramic assemblages are both functional and highly decorated. Archaeologists, of course, use decoration styles to identify and trace the movement of groups of people. They are able to do so for several reasons.

First, ceramic style is part of a larger design field that encompasses the decoration on such things as houses, drums, headdresses, basketry, beadwork, and the human body. Among groups that have been studied (for example Pedi, Tonga and Zulu), some 40 to 80 per cent of the total design fields also occur on pottery (Evers 1988). Some wall designs in Pedi courtyards, for example, can also be found on pots (Vogel 1985).

Similarly, some decorations on Zulu pots resemble slits made in human skin for medicines and have the same name (Mayr 1906). In the more distant past, designs on Zimbabwe-type stone walls also occurred on the associated pottery (see, for example, Robinson 1959). We can thus be confident that large design fields existed in the Early Iron Age even though only a portion has been preserved.

Secondly, the larger design field, including ceramic style, is the result of patterned behaviour created and learned by groups of people. This material culture style therefore distinguishes one group from another.

Thirdly, the creation of material-culture styles and their meanings must be at least partially accomplished through language. Because language is the principal vehicle for thinking about the world and transmitting those thoughts to others, there is a vital relationship between worldview, material culture, and language.

By tracing ceramic styles back through time, archaeologists have established the antiquity of present-day language groups. This is how we know that Eastern Bantu-speaking people dominated the Iron Age in southern Africa.

Among Eastern Bantu speakers, material-culture styles include a non-verbal code of communication that is significant to people within the group. In the case of pottery, this internal code is based on an association between pots and women. For example, an arc on a Zulu pot can represent the entrance to the great hut that, in turn, represents the womb (Berglund 1076:168). And among Shona, a special design on the neck/shoulder junction of a jar represents the beaded belt worn around a woman's waist to protect her fertility (Aquina 1968).

The stages of manufacture of Shona pottery also illustrate the fundamental relationship between women and pottery (Aschwanden 1982). Before firing, a pot is compared to a girl before puberty. If a young girl should walk where pot clay is dug up, or touch an unfired pot, the latent force within her (that will someday cause her first menstruation) will cause the pot to crack. Similarly, an adult woman will not make a pot while menstruating. A pot being fired is like a girl entering puberty, and if a man were to be present, the heat would be transferred to him and he would lose his virility. For similar reasons, a man should not be the first person to eat from a newly fired pot.

Because of this fundamental association, pots are a woman's weapon. Among Shona (Aschwanden 1982), one vessel in particular is associated with intercourse, and by placing it upside down a woman can deny her husband his conjugal rights. This example illustrates the active role of symbols in daily life.

Eastern Bantu speakers also use clay objects for symbolic purposes in various rituals and rites of passage. The most famous archaeological examples are seven hollow heads from the Early Iron Age site near Lydenburg (Inskeep and Maggs 1975; Maggs and Davidson 1981). These 'Lydenburg Heads' were made in the form of inverted pots with appliqué facial features and incised designs like those on the associated pottery.

THIS PAGE:
Lydenburg head (not original). Early Iron Age. (Collection: University of the Witwatersrand Archaeology Department)

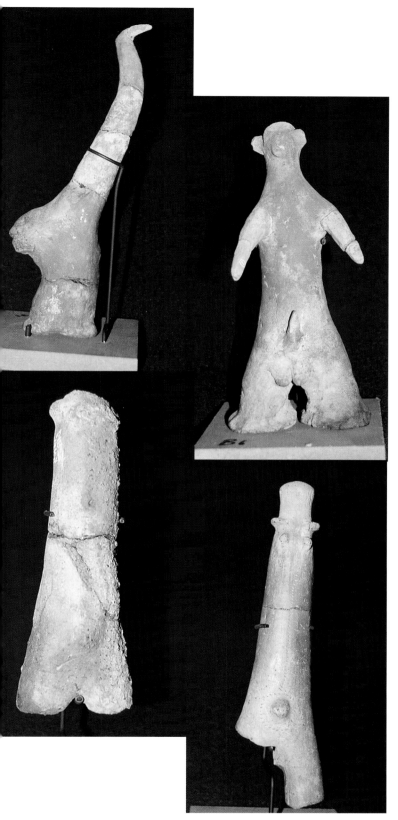

Two could have been worn as helmet masks, while the smaller heads may have been attached to a structure or a costume. They were probably all used in ritual dramas to mediate between the spirit world and everyday life. Other ritual objects have been found at the Middle Iron Age (AD900 to 1300) site of Schroda in the Shashe-Limpopo valley (Hanisch 1980). A hoard of some 400 figurine fragments was found in a special area near a cattle kraal. A line of posts divided the area into two zones. One contained mostly small, finely made figurines of domestic stock and small highly stylised human figures. The second zone contained larger, more crudely made figurines of wild animals, mythological creatures, and humans with animal characteristics. Caches of such unusual figurines inside a settlement are usually associated with initiation schools for girls. If the *domba* school of the Venda is a relevant analogy (see Nettleton 1984), then the Schroda figurines were probably used as props in lessons about proper moral behaviour and the structure of society. Similar caches have been found in Early Iron Age settlements in northern Zimbabwe (see, for example, Goodall 1960; Matenga 1993).

One type of female figurine in the Schroda hoard has a wide distribution in time and space. This figurine has well-rounded buttocks and clear breasts, but a phallic head (Summers 1957). According to a Lemba *nyanga* (traditional doctor), these figurines were made by young mothers as dolls for their daughters (Roumeguere and Roumeguere-Eberhardt 1960). At puberty, the girl's grandmother instructs her in the 'laws' of the doll, and later her husband must learn these laws as part of the marriage process.

Basically, the laws emphasise the patrilineal nature of Eastern Bantu life. The head is phallic because (as the law says): 'The head belongs to the father who conceived her.' The husband must respect his father-in-law who, along with his patrilineal ancestors, is the source of his wife's fertility. The husband obtains rights to this fertility through *lobola* (bridewealth in cattle), but he cannot own it. These ancient figurines are the forerunners of today's fertility dolls.

THIS PAGE:
Schroda figurines. Terracotta. Schroda site, Shashe-Limpopo valley. (Collection: National Cultural History Museum, Pretoria)

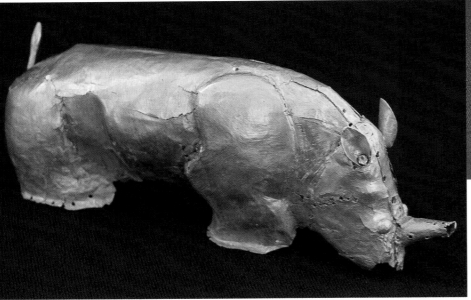

THIS PAGE, FROM LEFT:
Gold rhinoceros (original). Mapungubwe burial item;
Gold beaded necklace from royal burial site. Mapungubwe.
(Collection: SASOL African Heritage Exhibition housed at
the University of Pretoria)

Metal

Metal objects could also have symbolic significance. The most famous archaeological examples are the golden rhino from Mapungubwe, not far from Schroda in the Shashe-Limpopo valley.

Mapungubwe was the 13th-century capital of an African kingdom that was the forerunner to Great Zimbabwe. Indeed, Mapungubwe is the oldest place in southern Africa to reflect class distinction and sacred leadership – the hallmarks of a complex society.

In a cemetery on top of Mapungubwe there were some 23 graves, three of which included gold beads and bangles, a bowl and knobkerrie (or sceptre), and at least three rhino (Fouché 1937). The bowl, knobkerrie and rhino were made from gold sheeting tacked onto wooden cores. The rhino (particularly the black rhino) were probably symbols of leadership: like leaders, rhino were solitary, dangerous, and unpredictable. Even today, Shona and Venda people call the black rhino *chipembere* because of its similarity to a special dance (called *pembere*) that leaders perform at the graves of their ancestors (Huffman 1996).

The technology that produced the gold rhino at Mapungubwe was used much earlier for the production of iron and copper. Generally speaking, iron was associated with men and copper with women, and both were associated with procreation (Herbert 1984:19). Some iron furnaces were even modelled to look like the female body. Because women would be isolated when they give birth, furnaces should be located outside the settlement or in an otherwise secluded environment. By contrast, the forge was located in the village centre where the blacksmith hammered iron bloom into objects like hoes, axes, spears and knives. Copper was usually made into ornaments such as bangles and earrings.

Long-distance trade

Metal items were traded over long distances, especially to areas where ore was in short supply or to capitals involved in trade networks. The double iron gongs found at Thulamela in the Kruger Park, for example, probably came from Central Africa, and a tin ingot from the Rooiberg area in the North-West Province was found at Great Zimbabwe.

Long-distance networks were first established at the beginning of the Middle Iron Age, when Schroda was the capital in the Shashe-Limpopo valley. Besides the figurines, Schroda is important because it is the earliest Iron Age settlement in southern Africa with a substantial amount of locally made ivory objects and imported glass beads. These glass beads were imported from such places as Egypt and India, and Schroda was probably the first African capital in the interior to be integrated directly with the Indian Ocean commercial network.

Arab (see, for example, Freeman-Grenville 1975) and later Portuguese documents (see, for example, Barbosa, in Theal 1898:97) described the international extent of this trade. Ivory, gold, rhino horn and sometimes iron were taken to coastal stations in Mozambique, where they were loaded

on to Arab dhows and transported up the coast to the Swahili ports in East Africa that controlled the trade. After the goods were taxed, sailors followed the coast on monsoon winds to southern Arabia and India. There they traded the African goods for glass beads, glazed ceramics, and cotton and silk cloths. The traders returned on the reverse monsoon to East Africa, then sailed down the coast to start the cycle again.

This trade was taken over by the Portuguese in the 16th century. Dutch and British merchants later established new connections with different goods. One trade item, however, has remained popular throughout the last 1000 years.

Beads

Glass beads are the single most abundant import on Iron Age sites, and their distribution provides data for an analysis of the economic and political dynamics of the time. In the Shashe-Limpopo valley, for example, the chiefdom centred at Schroda gave way to a new group, called K2, after the archaeological name for the capital. So many glass beads flowed into the area that the K2 people melted them down and formed them into larger beads, it seems, to maintain their value. The resultant 'garden rollers' are among the earliest instances of glass reworking in Africa south of the Sahara (Gardner 1963; Wood 2000).

Many trade beads were made into simple strings, but others were worked into patterns on skins and cloths. One of the gold burials on Mapungubwe appears to have contained the earliest evidence of garments or girdles made of small beads (Fouché 1937). Satisfactory beadwork requires beads of equal size and shape, and small sizes are best (Wood 2000). The preference for small uniform beads today can be traced back to Mapungubwe.

Like pottery, beadwork styles today incorporate non-verbal codes meaningful to members of a particular group. In Zulu beadwork, for example, four designs (involving triangles in various combinations and orientations) refer to status: unmarried man, unmarried woman, married man and married woman (Mertens and Schoeman 1975). Significantly, these designs are also found on pots.

Conclusion

Traditional arts and crafts express the communal nature of African society. Craftspeople use a limited range of designs on multiple media to form material-culture styles that act as group signatures. Furthermore, everyone in the group can learn the symbolic meanings embedded in their crafts. These meanings are not individual statements, but are part of a network of associations fundamental to African society. This fundamental network, in turn, plays an active role in daily life. Symbols in action, networks of symbolic associations, and group styles help to provide the cultural context of traditional craft production.

today

It is not surprising to find young men and women from all cultural groups attending lectures on craft techniques and design theory, or learning craft skills from experts in their field at one of the many art schools or colleges. New materials and production techniques have moved craft far beyond the traditional methods practised by their grandparents, and yet those traditions survive side by side with the contemporary.

Craft has taken on an additional role as a means of earning a living. Craftspeople all over the world make handcrafted objects ranging from ceramics and glass through weaving and textiles, to jewellery and decorative objects. Consumers are attracted to products made by a specific craftsperson rather than an anonymous producer. The popularity of Carrol Boyes's metal products, Clemence Hwarire's basketry, or Anthony Shapiro's ceramic ranges, marketed as 'designer goods', are proof of this, as are the one-of-a-kind bone-china vessels cast and pierced by Martha Zettler. There is an appreciation of craftsmanship and good design in the highly technological 21st century, and an admiration for the time it takes to make products by hand or by semi-automated processes. Although not all craftspeople are in the same league as these, it does not prevent them from experiencing the satisfaction and excitement derived from creativity and a true love of their chosen material. As Peter Dormer observes in *The Culture of Craft*:

OPPOSITE PAGE:
Carrol Boyes. Napkin holder and platter.
Stainless steel, wood, aluminium and pewter.

THIS PAGE:
Martha Zettler. Bone-china vessels.

THIS PAGE, FROM LEFT:
Beverley Price. Necklaces. Beads, aluminum foil and laminated photostats of newspaper advertisements; Xhosa neckpiece or *amakhubalo*. Agapanthus roots, fibre. Below that, Xhosa nursing necklace or *ikhubalo*. Plastic spoons, beads.

'A set of values is associated with the freedom that comes through the possession of skills, the freedom that is attainable when one is in a position to direct the content, pace and quality of the way one earns a living.'

An expanding market catering for the needs of homeowners and interior designers has opened many doors for craftspeople who can supply ceramics, baskets, glass, fabrics, paper products, candles and an infinite variety of other objects. Hand-knitted and embroidered garments, woven scarves and wraps, which have always had their place at craft fairs and markets, have been joined by traditional tribal costumes adapted to contemporary wear and to up-market designer ranges including bags and hats.

Alongside the handcrafted silver and gold jewellery long created both in and out of Africa, we now find telephone-wire bangles and safety-pin collars, brightly coloured necklaces, bracelets and earrings worn as high fashion items. The traditional Zulu beaded love letter can now also send an AIDS awareness message, and fashion jewellery is based on traditional techniques but made from shiny beads and fashion colours, designed for the international market.

There is a universal attraction to the values associated with craft, in fact to handmade objects in general. It could be said that this is a result of the intellectual connection to historic eras or events that have a personal or symbolic meaning to the craftsman and are passed on to those who see and appreciate the object. It is the combination of

hand and mind in the making of craft objects that con-
nects us to the roots of mankind and to our cultural heritage, and the daily use of handmade objects that raises
the quality of life, as it has from the beginning of civilisation.
There is no particular reason why man must embellish and
decorate his surroundings and belongings but when one
sees a decorated wall or a door carved with exquisite sen-
sitivity it becomes apparent that we all need to see around
us the evidence of the creativity of others – or ourselves.

Although the number of objects we own has
increased enormously over the last few centuries, the
need for handmade objects has not diminished. The
energy and comfort that emanates from them is as
relevant today as it was millions of years ago.

a philosophy
of crafts

Muffin Stevens

A philosophy of crafts is concerned, among other ideas, with the meaning and social role of crafts. These have been different for different people and societies at different times in history. Western, Eastern and African ideas about crafts vary considerably, yet they share certain essential characteristics.

In the West, the 19th-century British designer, social reformer, craftsman and writer, William Morris, was influential in proposing, and working for a return to crafts after their decline during the Industrial Revolution. An astonishingly energetic and passionate man, he revived lost crafts like embroidery, stained glass, illumination and calligraphy, textile dyeing, printing and weaving, and high-warp tapestry, and pioneered a design style based on nature as an antidote to the alienation of city life. He believed strongly that the designer should not be separate from the maker, and wrote about 'joy in labour', hopeful that, if more industrial workers could be engaged in handcrafts, the quality of their lives would be improved. He matched this ideal with 'joy in use', the belief that the use of handmade objects was also healing and hopeful for the consumer. He famously wrote: 'Have nothing in your houses that you do not know to be useful, or believe to be beautiful.'

The legendary Indian statesman, philosopher, and activist, Mohandas Gandhi, the Mahatma (or 'Great Soul'), saw crafts as an essential part of authentic Indian life, a weapon in the Indian battle for independence from Great Britain, and a force for morality, spirituality and education. His Satyagraha campaign, developed on his return to India after many years in South Africa, was a campaign of non-violent resistance as a discipline of social struggle. Among other non-violent strategies, Satyagraha focused on redeveloping rural village crafts such as spinning and hand-weaving, ancient skills that Indian peasants had ceased to practice by the turn of the 20th century and which were almost extinct.

These became weapons in the struggle, with many potential benefits. One of these benefits was practical: without crafts, peasants were unemployed for four months of the year, and were so poor that even the smallest income from crafts would improve their lives. Secondly, the return to crafts was political, drawing attention to the appalling conditions in Indian villages that Gandhi wanted improved. Craft activities became symbolic of resistance to Western ways, British imperialism and modern industrialisation, as well as a means of achieving self-esteem and self-sufficiency. Gandhi proposed that all schools introduce productive

handcrafts into their curricula. Being as much a doer as a thinker, he himself practised spinning as a form of meditation, and trained villagers in leatherwork, pottery and textile crafts. His influence is still evident in present-day India, where crafts everywhere are made by ancient methods and are bought and used by Indians as much as by tourists, helping to keep craft traditions alive.

The British potter Bernard Leach developed a philosophy of crafts in the 20th century that, although focused on pottery, had an influence beyond the confines of that discipline. Born in China, Leach learnt pottery in Japan before setting up a studio in England. He was much inspired by Japanese ideas about crafts, which are so highly regarded there that great craftspeople are declared National Living Treasures, and crafts are as important as fine arts. Leach felt that the East had preserved vital, living traditions on which contemporary crafts could be built, whereas the West had lost these because of the development of industry and the substitution of machine-made for man-made goods. Leach found much to emulate and admire in Japan, but also looked to pre-industrial Europe, and aimed for a synthesis of East and West in his philosophy. He felt that beauty was

to be found in the simple use of natural materials, and considered technique merely a means to an end. He believed in an intuitive and honest approach to design and making, as opposed to a rigidly rational or mechanical one, and in utility as the first principle of beauty. Utility, combined with subtle decoration derived from established traditions, would, he felt, enable the craftsperson to produce craft objects that appeal to and are understood through the senses.

In Africa a multiplicity of different craft traditions exists, so there is little purpose in generalising about them. However, there has traditionally been no clear distinction between fine art and craft. African artefacts usually had both an aesthetic and a utilitarian dimension, and were made for tribal and communal purposes, and not primarily as objects

of individual expression. Such crafted objects were very much part of people's lives and belief systems and are complex cultural expressions.

Materials used were generally locally available, although certain imported substances, like glass beads, became very important. Advanced techniques and technologies were carried over from one generation to another, usually by systems of apprenticeship under a master craftsman or within family businesses. The objects produced generally had powerful formal, decorative and symbolic qualities.

While many craft objects were and are made for everyday use in tribal life, other objects and materials are particularly highly regarded for their visual and aesthetic qualities, which, in turn, become important in ritual, spiritual and social practices. For example, glass beads are worked into jewellery, clothing and masks, all of which are treasured as dowries, heirlooms and carriers of wealth; decorated calabashes, with no utilitarian function, are valued by Wodaabe women as signs of status and display; in traditional Benin culture, red coral, cloth and bronzes are so powerful because of their colour that they are deemed dangerous and are subject to strong taboos. Many African crafts are

highly decorated, with complex abstract and representational signs that send messages, tell stories, record histories, reflect beliefs and express power.

As tribal lifestyles have changed, these traditional arts and the indigenous knowledge systems underlying them have also changed, producing artefacts with different purposes for different audiences, such as curios, popular art and tourist art, as well as individually conceived art or craft objects. Thus in South Africa, at present, crafts may take a multitude of directions, while fulfilling a variety of social roles and giving rise to multiple meanings.

tomorrow

Through craft training programmes, groups of women now have the skills and the materials to make and market many interesting handmade products, giving them the pride of knowing that they have earned money to feed their children. They have been empowered to assist their communities with the knowledge to inform them about HIV/AIDS and the devastation that it can cause families.

Many communities with traditional craft skills lacked the means to translate their skills into products with market potential, but, with workshops on marketing and business skills, product development and other relevant topics, productivity and capacity are constantly improving. The results are evident in the many new products reaching the market, ranging from wonderful Christmas decorations to bags and cushion covers, baskets and mats, printed fabrics and beaded clothing. It has become possible for people to earn a sustainable income from the craft objects they can make, while remaining close to their homes and their children, bringing hope and a viable future to many families.

The interest in all things South African that was revived when the country rejoined the community of nations in the 1990s has played an important role in the development of the local craft industry. Markets in the tourism and eco-tourism industry have expanded and will continue to do so. The inclusion of craft into the interiors of homes, hotels, restaurants and offices has expanded the market

OPPOSITE PAGE:
Zulu beer pots and porcupine quills. Interior by Wilson and Associates, South Africa. Intercontinental. Airport Hotel, Johannesburg (Photograph by Frances Janisch, NY)

THIS PAGE:
Sue Meyer and **Nelius Britz**. Cast glass. Nautical steel fittings. Western Cape Hotel. Arabella Country Estate.

for handmade products, while homeware stores and decorating magazines have popularised the use of 'the object.' Homeowners are just as likely to buy a basket or a cloth to hang on a wall as a print or painting, making crafts a much sought after commodity.

The recognition by the South African government of craft as a cultural industry with growth potential has given the craft industry a boost, and the general buzz of creativity all over the country has led to the formation of numerous craft groups. Some gather around church structures or schools or recreation centres, others are born of shared problems, such as HIV/AIDS, physical disabilities or unemployment. Yet others form among people with common or complementary skills who create outstanding craft objects. Small businesses employ skilled craftspeople for specific jobs, such as throwing pots or carving, carpet weaving or basket making. There is a growing awareness of the opportunities offered by crafts for job creation and poverty alleviation.

THIS PAGE, FROM LEFT:
Sue Jowell. Mirror. Kim Sacks Gallery;
Barbara Jackson. Ceramic vessel.

OPPOSITE PAGE:
Traditonal Zulu 'isixholo' hats from Zululand, Kwazulu Natal. Interior Design by Wilson and Associates, South Africa (Photograph by David Ross).

about this book

The biennial *FNB Vita Craft Now Exhibition* was the spark that inspired us to write this book. The first major craft exhibition, held in 1993 at the Johannesburg Art Gallery, attracted the attention of First National Bank who, impressed by the skill and technique on display, offered to fund a biennial exhibition and award prizes to the best craft objects. The appeal of the exhibition has been universal. It has expanded in size and scope, including a series of regional and specialist exhibitions, and become an important showcase for both new and established craftspeople. Through intensive nationwide publicity, craftspeople all over the country are encouraged to submit photographs of their work for selection – a process that has gathered momentum over the years. The result has been a flood of creativity that we believe should be recorded and publicised.

Having worked in the craft community for many years, we are constantly amazed and delighted by the extent of the creativity we have found, and by the ability of people to make objects of beauty from found materials, whether natural, such as reed, grass and clay, or synthetic, such as telephone wire and plastic bags. We experience a sense of wonder when we see a puppet carefully made from wood and fabric, or touch a basket woven from softly coloured grasses into a form that is volumetric but light, resilient and strong. It is the combination of shape, colour and form, combined with the visual and tactile excitement of the surface that makes craft unique. We hope, through this book, to pass this excitement on to the reader and bring the wide range of crafts and craftspeople in South Africa to an audience of craft lovers.

OPPOSITE PAGE, FROM LEFT:
Mapula Embroidery Project. 2000 *FNB Vita Craft Now Exhibition* winners.

THIS PAGE:
Julius Mfethe. Carved wooden figures. 1997 *FNB Vita Craft Now Exhibition* winner.

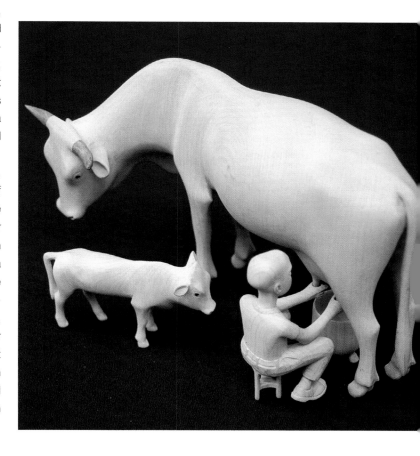

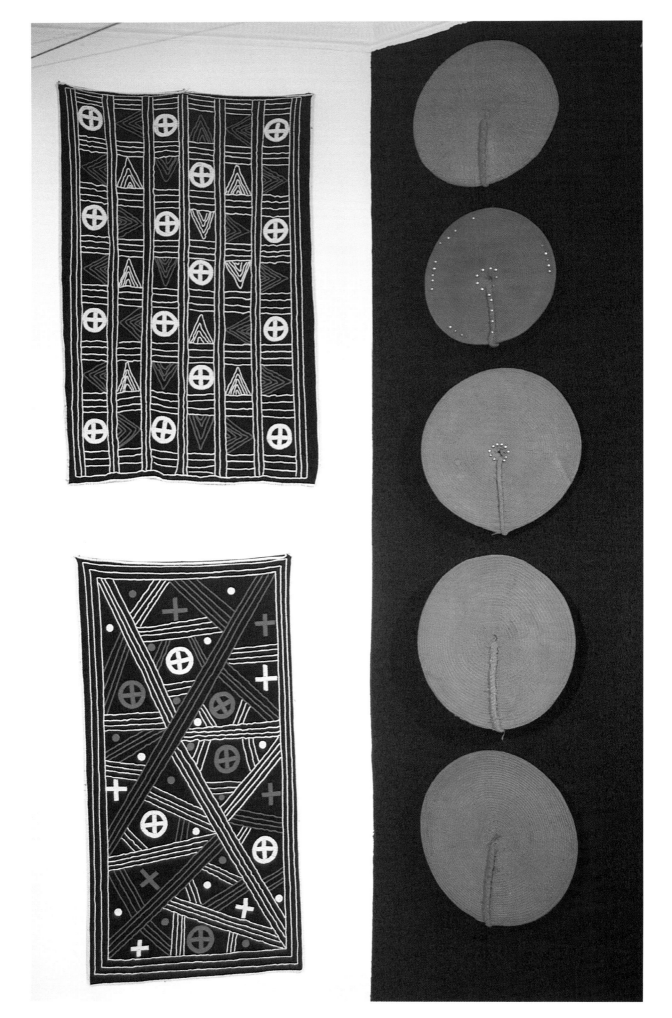

structure

We have divided the book into three sections – 'Traditional', 'Transitional' and 'Contemporary'.

- 'Traditional' covers crafts created using techniques passed down through the generations to make objects for daily or ceremonial use – objects that are frequently sought after by collectors and museums.

- 'Transitional' includes crafts made by using traditional techniques, skills or materials to develop a new range of objects. The creative process of using known skills and readily available materials to design and produce new products is a natural one that has resulted in development and progress. An example in South Africa is the use of plastic beads in traditional beadwork, or telephone wire for basket making. New materials excite creative people and inspire them to make new products. It should be noted that the concept of 'transitional' is not used with art historic reference or to suggest a time frame.

OPPOSITE PAGE:
Zulu hats or *inhloko*. On wall of Kim Sacks Gallery.
Billy Makubele and family, Tsonga embroidered cloths. Fabric, threads and beads. Kim Sacks Gallery.

THIS PAGE, FROM LEFT:
Two wooden Tsonga headrests or *xikhigelo*. (Collection: Standard Bank Foundation of African Art, housed at the University of the Witwatersrand Art Galleries); **Sue Meyer**. Dancing Headrest: *pâte de verre*. As a former dancer with the Royal Ballet Company, her 'dancing' headrest shows the movement and flow of ballet combined with the form of a traditional headrest.

- 'Contemporary' covers the rapidly developing field of designer items, frequently the work of formally trained professionals, that is becoming a manufacturing sector of note in South Africa. We also use the term to denote one-of-a-kind objects that edge into the field of art.

In addition, we have included profiles on craftspeople and insets by experts or information on interesting topics:

- The nature of a particular craft, like that of all creative endeavours, is intimately linked to the individuals who create it. We felt it appropriate to focus on some of these individuals, profiling them, discussing their ideas, and showing examples of their work and lifestyle.

- Varied aspects of craft have been written about by experts in their field, giving a wider dimension to the book's content.

Just as the distinctions between art and craft in Africa have become blurred, and lines have been crossed and re-crossed, we ask that the divisions in this book be seen as boundaries that can be crossed in any direction. There is such a wealth of innovation and individual creative design in the craft arena that it is impossible to place every object neatly in a chapter or section. Their position in the book is sometimes a result of the rough rules we have laid down as a means of dividing the book up and sometimes a factor of a connection with other crafts in a particular section. The intention is to show the links between traditional crafts and inventive new products, to demonstrate the many different ways the same material can be used in different crafts, and to illustrate the South African style that is steadily emerging and enriching all who share a passion for beautiful things made with care and dedication by talented people.

traditional

Sitting under a marula tree in Venda, where the road turns to the north towards Rebecca Matibe's house, is a group of drum makers slowly chipping away with an *adze* as they make large ceremonial drums. The wooden drums of the Venda are made from a 'slice' of tree cut from the forests up in the sacred mountains. The diameter of the tree dictates the size of the drum and the 'crossed rope' handles, carved from the corners of the slab, are used to suspend the drum so that it is easier to play. A well-cured cowhide, which has lain in the dam for a length of time before being stretched and smoothed, is used over the drum mouth.

The sound of the very large drums is deafening and can be heard rolling through the sacred mountains. The drums may only be played at the command of the rulers and are not only used to make music, but are also said to have magical properties, such as the ability to drum up lightning and rain. Smaller drums beat out the rhythm for the dances performed for initiation ceremonies and other traditional rites.

South Africa has a heritage of craft production, passed down through families and ethnic groups. Traditional craft objects were made by hand from available materials, such as clay, fibre, wood and metal, for specific functions within the community – whether domestic, secular, sacred or ceremonial.

Pots were made spherical for strength so they could be used for transporting water, for storage, or for cooking and for serving food; baskets were made volumetric for carrying and gathering, and round – with a lid – for storing seeds and herbs, while carved sticks were made for ceremonies, defence, or simply for support. There were sleeping mats and headrests, woven cloths for garments and covers, wooden bowls, decorative and symbolic beadwork, weapons and tools and many, many other handmade items in daily use.

Most of the domestic objects were made by women, while men concentrated on the weapons, tools and musical instruments of their culture. Frequently, the maker would embellish the object with ritualistic or symbolic patterning carved, burned or scratched into it, or painted, drawn or embroidered on its surface. Soft fabrics and basket fibres were often dyed with natural plant materials then woven to form patterning. Originally patterns on domestic and other objects were determined by tradition or used as identification of place or family or perhaps, even, to convey messages, such as those of the beaded love letters of the Zulu people. Later, personal skills led to particular styles, specific to individuals and localised groups.

Globalisation has, however, brought with it the possibility that manufacturers may now mass produce traditional craft and flood the markets, so research is being done into traditional knowledge systems and ways to protect the intellectual property of individuals, communities and ethnic groups. This is vital if the skills and methods of craft making, and the symbolism of the decoration are to be protected and conserved.

This section focuses on outstanding craftspeople who are custodians of heritage by virtue of their use of traditional techniques and materials in spite of all the changes in the modern world. In some instances, the skills have been lost and then rediscovered, or reinvented from the objects still around.

THIS PAGE, FROM TOP:
Traditional Zulu pot; Drum maker. Venda.

OPPOSITE PAGE, FROM TOP:
Traditional Venda pots; Married woman's apron or liphotho. Detail. Hide and beads.

the heritage of craft

Maleleke Frank Ledimo
Senior Curator, University of the Witwatersrand Art Galleries

For a nation to forge its own identity, it is important to understand its past. After the demise of apartheid in South Africa in 1994, there dawned an era within which South Africa has had to reposition herself not only globally, but within the African continent. Her past led to international isolation and created an oppressive environment where diverse cultural, religious and political beliefs and opinions were suppressed and outlawed. The new era calls her to reinvent herself within the paradigm of the African Renaissance, as can be seen in southern Africa through the regional cooperation of the Southern African Development Countries (SADC). The significant role that arts, culture and heritage can play in reshaping this new era cannot, therefore, be ignored.

THIS PAGE, FROM LEFT:
Doorway at Basotho Cultural Village;
Decorated mud wall with pebble inclusions.

OPPOSITE PAGE:
Entrances to traditional huts.

the cultural
importance of craft
in South Africa

Human beings tend to base their identity on associations with particular (tribal) groups and, as a result, this is often manifest in showing some sort of allegiance to those groups. In Africa and Asia, for example, this is even marked with facial and bodily scarifications. This self-identification could also be reflected through costume and dress (especially during wars). Other ways include braiding hair, body painting, architectural style, traditional house decorations, symbols, colours and patterns. These elements were also transposed in the designs of craft 'products', making them an important way in which people make self-identifications.

The KhoiSan's stone tools, their rock art, clothing, and hunting tools, such as the bow and arrow, are some of the earliest known 'crafts' produced in southern Africa. Embedded in African thought or philosophy and literature is a universal African belief purported by traditions of oral history and storytelling. This history has in it stories of heroes and heroines, villains and monsters, rolling hills and events of the past, and these are often incorporated in the designs, symbols and motifs in craft production. The archaeological findings at Mapungubwe, the remains of which provide evidence of early human settlement at various sites in the area, tell a story of early kingdoms and nations that lived long before the arrival of European settlers. Through these artefacts, we are able to establish the time that this dynasty existed.

Craft production under apartheid was interrupted by the migrant labour system – despite the fact that most of the craft was produced by women, who stayed behind while their husbands went off to work in South Africa's mines. The 'development' of craft under missionaries – as a way of vocational training – had some significance, but it was often void of cultural significance or pagan symbols and, as a result, mainly utilitarian objects were made. Craft today is equally linked to indigenous knowledge systems: the making of the deadly KhoiSan bow and arrow, the thunderous spiritual drum, the grass baskets that are able to hold beer and keep it cool – all are a reflection of African indigenous ingenuity. All these illustrate the significance of craft in providing us with some knowledge of the way traditional African people lived. The Mapungubwe findings also tell us of the technological know-how of smelting and manipulating metal such as gold.

Traditionally, the business of making craft was left to the carver, the potter and the maker, who enjoyed considerable status in the community. It was believed that the maker had a 'calling' – much like that of the traditional healer – to carve and produce these objects; disregarding this 'calling' would result in them becoming mentally and spiritually ill. The crafters usually produced objects as per their client's request.

Traditionally, production of these artefacts or decorative objects was linked to their utilitarian application or symbolic use. They could be used as gifts, as ornaments and family heirlooms. At the occasion of ancestors being 'invited' to a new homestead, beer would be brewed and served in specially made clay pots. Lovers exchanged their vows at a community gathering, with ornaments such as love letters made of coloured beads. The bride would be given a specially made broom for her to keep her new homestead symbolically 'clean'. The activity of doing or making craft in Africa is, thus, a very important sociocultural activity that represents various stages of human life.

African society and the African universe often have different stages that need to be observed through ceremonies and rituals, and craft has been used to mark all these in the full circle of life – from birth, during various rites of passage, to the end of life or death, the celebration of the ancestors (*badimo* or *izinyanya*) and the journey into the afterworld. Craft objects are, however, also used for personal ornamentation, in earrings, finger rings, necklaces, bracelets

and other decorative jewels. These are often worn on the head or forehead and include objects of rituals, such as ceremonial masks, while musical percussions are worn around ankles. The drum beat of *sangomas* or *inyangas* is used to evoke and call ancestors, while their white beads signify a purity that helps connect with ancestors in the afterworld.

Colour has important symbolism: white is seen as a reflection of clarity (a *sangoma* initiate is led to the river by a white beetle, after which he or she has to wear white beads), while black is a rather ambiguous colour as it has both evil and good associations. Black marks the mourning period and the darkness of the night when evil acts are committed, but it is also a sign of fertility: the black of the soil and 'black' clouds will help yield good crops. Blue and green are often interchanged and symbolise wealth and prosperity, manifest in green plants or crops. The colour red signals danger, as it is the colour of blood and fire. Most of these colours are thus incorporated into beadwork, basket designs and other craft objects that clearly form a noteworthy part of the African universe.

Today, the sale of craft to the general public has increased tremendously, and this is due largely to a return to traditional cultural values. Significantly, the resurgence of flea markets, expositions, craft competitions, craft training centres and crafts linked to SMME (Small, Medium and Micro Enterprises) development have all contributed to the growth of craft. It is also trendy today for celebrities to wear traditional craft ornaments. Companies are giving craft objects as corporate gifts and commissioning crafters to make objects for their

THIS PAGE, FROM LEFT:
Broom in Noria Mabasa's house, Venda; Ndebele bridal train or *inyoga*. Beads. (Collection: Standard Bank Foundation of African Art, housed at the University of the Witwatersrand Art Galleries)

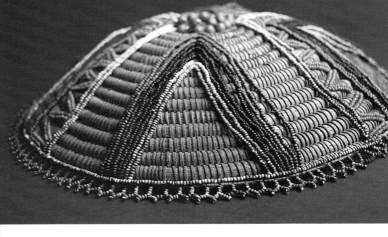

boardrooms. Another important sector that has played a significant role in this development is the contribution made by museums, galleries and private collections, such as the superb craft objects that are part of the Brenthurst Collection at the Johannesburg Art Gallery.

It is important to note that production of craft was and still is important in the lives of traditional urban and rural people. Symbols, colours, patterns and motifs are used to represent a clan, and much attention is given to detail of design and the rendering of surfaces, while at the same time keeping their simplicity. These elements of craft are also used to tell family histories – each piece appears to be mystical, taking one through time and space – and may reflect land, wealth and the status in the community of those for whom the object is made.

With the increase in urbanisation and forced migration, a number of innovations and adaptations have taken place in craft production. These have resulted in changes in design, the materials used and the object's utility or use. Designs and motifs tend to have less symbolism, and materials such as wire and a variety of 'found materials' are now used. It has also been interesting to see traditional clay pots being used as decorative pots for plants and not to brew or serve beer. A vibrant adaptation of traditional grass-weaving techniques is to use telephone wire to weave *imbenge* bowls and spoons, and this has become so popular that these objects are fast becoming collectors' items. Unlike grass, items made from telephone wire have more colour and their pattern combinations are more striking, contributing further to their popularity.

A wide variety of craft objects are nevertheless still being produced in a traditional setting and to a required standard. *Ukhamba* (beer baskets) are bulb-shaped containers rendered watertight by the density of the coil-weave, and the material used is usually the ilala palm. These baskets are traditionally used to serve *umgqombothi* or sorghum beer during ritual or

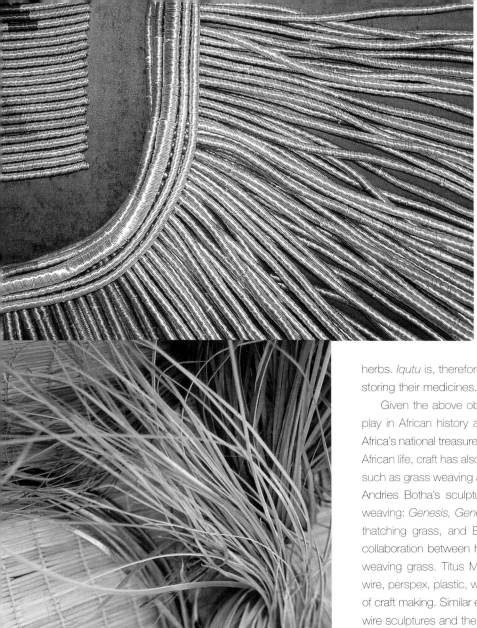

ceremonial occasions. The *isiquabetho* or open bowl is a large basin-shaped basket, which is traditionally used for gathering and carrying grain. It is used in modern times as a fruit bowl or grouped decoratively on a wall. *Iqutu* (herb baskets) are the smallest of the Zulu baskets, which – unlike *ukhamba* – are usually loosely woven because they are used for storing food, especially dried herbs. *Iqutu* is, therefore, popular among *sangomas*, who use it for storing their medicines.

Given the above observations, craft clearly has a salient role to play in African history and, as such, is an important part of South Africa's national treasure and cultural heritage. In contemporary South African life, craft has also influenced the visual arts, where techniques such as grass weaving and beadwork have been incorporated in art. Andries Botha's sculptures incorporate traditional cane and grass weaving: *Genesis, Genesis, Jesus* (1990) is made of leadwood and thatching grass, and Botha acknowledges that this piece was a collaboration between himself and a group of women working with weaving grass. Titus Moteyane's *Concorde*, which is made of tin, wire, perspex, plastic, wheels and pigment, lends it technique to that of craft making. Similar elements are seen in Walter Oltmann's brass-wire sculptures and the paintings of Alexis Preller – the latter's series of *The Grand Mapogga* (1957) has as its subject matter several colourful abstract portraits inspired by an Ndebele figure.

It is hoped that craft production will continue to grow through the support of the private and public sector. The market is slowly widening, both at home and abroad, and the opportunity exists for craft to play a vital role in the African Renaissance. Like any other cultural or heritage activity that attracts tourists, craft is in itself a golden prospect, and the establishment of shops, curio outlets, flea markets and craft emporia allow for an even brighter future. Having said that, it is important to attach meaning to these objects by knowing how and why they are made. In this way, they become objects that can be appreciated more and with greater pride.

makers

basket
weavers

Baskets – easy to carry, strong, pliable and spacious – are extremely versatile and can be used for carrying and gathering crops or for bringing produce home from the market, while the lidded variety are used for storage and the flattish ones as chaffing baskets. Almost any pliable materials, from soft branches and grass to palm fronds and even plastic and telephone wire can be used to weave a basket. Various techniques determine the shape and size of the basket, which is often made for a specific use according to the customs and needs of the community. The Tsonga marriage baskets – made to keep the ceremonial food clean and warm – are covered in beads to emphasise the importance of the ceremony. The lid or *xintewana* is made by one family and the bottom or *xinthabana* by the other to signify the coming together of two families.

Basket making is widely spread throughout the country, but KwaZulu-Natal is really the leader in this field. This is partly because, until recently, crafts were still taught in primary schools throughout the province, thus developing and sustaining a strong craft tradition. Another reason is that there is an abundance of grass types suitable for basket making on the hills of Zululand, while ilala palm from the coastal regions is brought into the area by truck and sold to the weavers.

OPPOSITE PAGE:
Tsonga-Shangaan. Beads and fibre. Marriage baskets. The top is the *xintewana* and the base, *xithabana*. (Collection: Audrey Coleman)

THIS PAGE, FROM TOP:
Basedi ba Bapedi. Woman with traditional woven baskets from Limpopo; Detail of basket by **Reuben Ndwandwe**; Detail of basket by **Edna Nxgonga**.

Traditional *izicephu* or sitting mats and *amacansi* or sleeping mats are made from sedges such as *incema,* and are decorated with embroidery or dyed patterns. The lidded baskets, originally used for the storage of beer and food, are made from the ilala palm. They had very simple designs, but new patterns and colours have recently been introduced to satisfy the many keen customers. Making these spectacular baskets is very labour intensive and time-consuming, as thin strips of ilala palm have to be wrapped around coils of grass and sewn together in a spiral fashion. The design is created by using several different colours that are woven in zigzags around the basket.

The story goes that, about 25 years ago, local basket-making traditions had virtually been lost, but the concerted efforts of Elliot 'Baba' Dludla, who was making shopping baskets for the Johannesburg market, Ben Sikosana – who brought people together from various parts of Zululand – and a Swedish missionary reintroduced the skills to groups of craftspeople from all over Northern KwaZulu-Natal, and Vukani – a basket cooperative – was established for marketing the products. Baba Dludla, who claims to have learnt the skills handed down through generations from an old woman in his church in about 1942, was a key figure in the project, and it is he who has kept Vukani together to this day.

traditional basket weavers

Reuben Ndwandwe and Beauty Nxgonga

Reuben Ndwandwe is a renowned basket weaver and one of the few men still making baskets. He makes finely woven open bowls or *imbenge* (used to cover the beer pots) and round, lidded *ukhamba* using an unusual colour combination – including a soft lilac tone combined with shades of brown and tan – and a unique method of weaving that has a raised pattern woven over the base colour.

Reuben developed this technique when he contracted tuberculosis and was admitted to Hlabisa Hospital. While there, he had nothing to do, so he asked if he could weave baskets from ilala palm and various grasses. Because he could not obtain the dyes he liked to use, the baskets were decorated with a pattern using the grass alone. After he was discharged, he used unusual colours made from roots, berries and leaves to dye the grass and ilala palm. He learnt the techniques of basket making from his mother and grandmother, and has now taught his wife and some of his 11 children to continue the tradition.

Reuben was born in Hlabisa, KwaZulu-Natal, and was an early contributor to the Vukani Association in Eshowe. He has exhibited widely and won a prize in the Small Basket category at the Basket Exhibition held in 1996 at the African Art Centre in Durban. In 1997, he had work on display at the *FNB Vita Craft Exhibition* held in Pretoria, and his work is represented in many public and private collections both locally and overseas.

Beauty Nxgonga is one of the best-known basket-makers in KwaZulu-Natal. She works with her daughter Edna in the Hlabisa region near the Hluhluwe game reserve. Her large, narrow-necked baskets, known as *isichumo*, are woven very tightly with vibrant designs created by dyeing the ilala palm with a variety of colours obtained from leaves, bark and roots, and even rusty tins, according to old family recipes. Beauty started weaving baskets in 1983 after she learnt the technique from her mother, but it is her friend, Lorentia Dlamini, who taught her to weave using the folioles of the ilala palm wrapped around coils of grass and sewn together in a spiral fashion.

Beauty creates the designs for her baskets as she works, gauging the diameter so the design fits exactly. Her references and inspiration come from her surroundings, giving the baskets a regional and family identity. She and Edna do not plan the designs but develop them as they work, resulting in baskets with an integrity and perfection that are quite unique. Each basket can take up to two weeks to complete.

pottery makers

Women with pots carefully balanced on their heads, wending their way to the river to collect water for their households, are a common sight in Africa. Pottery is still made and used daily, as it was in times gone by. The volumetric forms, made in the traditional coiling or scraping methods, create an archetypal rounded pot that balances on a small foot or on a grass ring so that it may be carried on the head. Sometimes a neck is added, which – apart from adding reinforcement to the rim – prevents the liquid from splashing out when walking. Because of the rounded form and the coarse grain of the clay, pots can withstand direct heat from a fire and can thus be used for cooking. They are also used for storage and for brewing the communal beer, for drinking and eating and, in certain instances, for ceremonies and rituals.

The clay is dug from the river beds and known sites in the hills, and prepared by first taking out the larger stones and sticks and then grinding it with a stone in a similar manner to that of grinding corn. The fine, powdered clay is slaked in water and then kneaded or wedged in preparation for the potter to coil the pots – as it has been done for millennia.

A few years ago, a seminal exhibition of traditional South African pottery, entitled *Emhlabeni – From the Earth* and curated by members of the University of the Witwatersrand, aimed to show continuity and change, old forms and new content. Fiona Rankin-Smith discussed the exhibition in an accompanying document (See right):

OPPOSITE PAGE:
Rebecca Matibe. Ceramic and graphite vessel with snake and bird decorations.

THIS PAGE:
Rebecca Matibe's homestead in Venda with ceramic and graphite pots in the foreground.

'Clay pots are frequently regarded as simply utilitarian, yet the meanings associated with the process of making as well as the objects themselves can shift that understanding. The transformations that occur when formless earth is beaten, pounded, shaped by human hands (without a wheel) and made permanent through firing has been interpreted as a metaphor for life, the processes equalling the various stages an individual must pass through in order to reach maturity. Extending the analogy – pottery can reflect aspects of the social and ritual circumstances in a community, pots have been buried with the dead and broken shards placed on shrines as part of a sacred rite. Clay pots feature in numerous ceremonies and a vessel can become a meeting place for spirits. Throughout South Africa, beer pots are not only functional, but when not in use are left slightly uncovered in a dark, cool place to allow the ancestors access.'

traditional
potters

Rebecca Matibe
and Nesta Nala

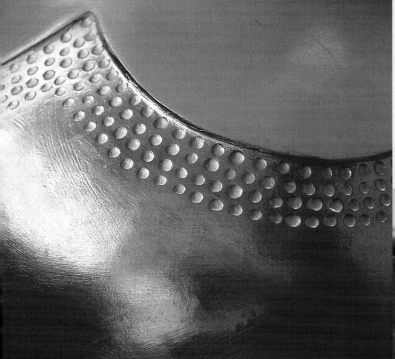

Rebecca Matibe is a traditional potter from Venda, in the far northeast of the country. She works in a thatched rondavel that leads out onto a walled patio. The low surrounding walls are painted in traditional patterns, and the floor is treated with a mix of clay and cow dung that forms a shiny surface when dry. A pattern is combed into the mixture when it is still wet, giving a soft texture to the floor.

Rebecca sits on the ground, dressed in her traditional clothes, working between her outstretched legs. She uses clay from a deposit to the south, close to the pot-making Mashamba Village. The pot is formed from a thick, flattened coil that is joined and smoothed into a doughnut form, and then scraped up from the inside with the fingers of one hand while the other supports the outside. The top of the pot is formed first and finished neatly at the rim with a coil that is smoothed using a small clay slip-soaked sponge. When the pot is leather hard, it is turned over and the bottom is scraped inwards until it is closed and perfectly rounded. If a larger pot is required, further coils are added before the rim is made.

Rebecca learned to make cooking pots from her grandmother, but after she married, her sister-in-marriage – one of her husband's four chosen wives, who was a potter – taught her further pottery skills. Rebecca realised she had a talent for this craft and extended her skills to make pots needed in the daily life of her village as well as individual pots sought by collectors from all over the world.

The small rounded pots Rebecca makes are used in the community for cooking, while the larger pots are made for grain and water storage, and for beer brewing. Her own water container is almost a metre in diameter and the grain is stored in yet another enormous pot beside her house. In addition to her traditional forms are large pots decorated with her own imagery. She models birds on the rims of the pots or nesting on the side, while snakes entwine the handles and threaten the birds or other creatures on the surface. The pots are made of bright terracotta clay decorated with bands or chevrons of graphite, which she burnishes with a treasured smooth stone. This combination of graphite on terracotta clay is particular to the people of Venda.

Rebecca has seven children, four girls and three boys, all of whom were educated with the help of the profits from the pottery. The youngest of Rebecca's children – Pferrelo Lucky Matibe – has chosen to join his mother as a potter, so the skills will be passed on to yet another generation. Technikon art students and fellow craftspeople have also been taught these

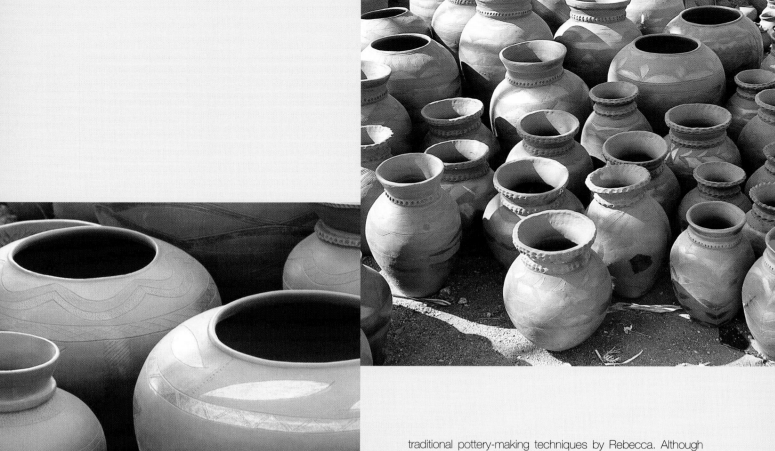

CLOCKWISE, FROM LEFT:
Mashamba Village. Venda. Terracotta pots; **Nesta Nala**. Large pot with raised decorations or *amasumpa*. 1995 FNB Vita Craft Now Exhibition winner; **Jabu Nala**. Burnished and decorated terracotta pot.

traditional pottery-making techniques by Rebecca. Although she speaks very little English, her daughter and manager, Alice Netshidzivhani, is always willing to translate for her. They have opened a craft shop on the main road close to Thohoyandou – the largest city in the area – and sell Rebecca's pots as well as the work of other craftspeople in the vicinity.

At Mashamba, Rebecca has helped to teach the women from the community to make not only larger pots than they used to, but also a wider variety of forms and decorations. The women of this village have made domestic pots for many generations and have now been given a large shed so they are no longer dependent on good weather for the pot-making schedule. They have gone into production and are making garden pots and even water features in traditional terracotta and graphite.

Nesta Nala is a Zulu potter renowned for the perfect, simple, round, black pots she makes at her home in Oyaya in the Kranzkop area of KwaZulu-Natal.

Nesta coils her thin-walled pots from the base upwards, finishing the top rim with her fingers. The pots are decorated with added rope-like coils and clay pellets, or *amasumpa*, representing the cattle so important to the Nguni people. In 1983, an archaeologist working in the area showed Nesta shards of Early Iron Age pots found in the region and

suggested that she use the ancient designs, which she now incorporates into her distinctive pots.

Although both Rebecca and Nesta use similar techniques to make their pots, Nesta needs her pots to be black and glossy, so she fires them in a pit-fired kiln using aloe leaves and cow dung to achieve the reduction atmosphere. Rebecca, on the other hand, needs a more open fire that keeps the brightness of the terracotta clay and the burnished graphite.

The tradition of passing craft skills to family members and from mother to daughter continues today, although there is always the temptation to leave the rural areas for the cities. Nesta, who learnt pottery making from her mother Sephiwe, has five daughters – Jabu, Thembi, Zanele, Nonhlanhla and Bongi – all of whom are potters. They all return to their home to collect clay – even Jabu, who comes from Johannesburg, six hours away. Close by, the Magwaza family of 13 potters – sisters, sisters-in-law and daughters, all making outstanding pots for both the domestic and tourism markets – also work within a family unit.

woodcarvers

Traditionally, men never went on a journey without their sticks – often beautifully carved with patterns, figures, feet or animals and reptiles. Sticks are still used for hunting as well as walking, and are very personal possessions. The symbolism and style of carving can denote the social group of the owner, his status and so on, but many of the woodworkers have pushed the boundaries of their creativity and have come up with altered products.

Woodcarving is among the oldest and most developed crafts in Africa. A wide variety of indigenous trees provide wood in many colours, strengths and hardnesses, which are made into traditional objects for regular use in homesteads: sticks, knobkerries, stools, wheels, bowls, doors, milk pails, meat platters with carved or engraved handles, wooden spoons and utensils, containers and many other utilitarian objects. Headrests decorated with great attention to detail were used to protect the elaborate hairstyle of the sleeping owner. Although they are still made, they are not commonly used, but may sometimes be slept on in order to contact the spirit of the original owner.

The doors of rulers and elders are often elaborately decorated with symbolic patterns to denote status within the community, or carved with protective symbols to keep the occupants of the house safe from harm. The doors of the villagers are usually less elaborate, but may also be carved with protective symbolism.

Wooden objects are carved or chipped out of wood, with details burnt into the surface using a hot poker, or scratched, smoothed and chiselled using a variety of tools. The decoration can be quite minimal and carefully rounded, or it can be rich with patterns and symbols. Many of these techniques are still used today with outstanding skill and to great effect.

OPPOSITE PAGE:
Kromkloof Group. Decorated wooden bowl. Wire and beads. Designs burnt onto the wooden surface; Traditional wooden meat platter. (Collection: Karel Nel)

THIS PAGE, FROM TOP:
Carved Venda door or *makumbane*. Detail.
Traditional meat platter. (Collection: Karel Nel); **Kromkloof Group**. Open wooden bowl with burnt design.

wall painters

The rolling grasslands of the Free State towards the Drakensberg mountains were once scattered with traditional homesteads that were plastered with clay from the rivers and inscribed with wonderful patterns and designs. Sometimes, the clay was of various earth tones, but was usually simply patterned with a comb in a formalised design derived from plants or flowers. The women began the craft of wall painting when mud walls replaced the reed fences that were used to divide the courtyards in traditional homesteads. These techniques have only been used for about the last 100 years and are, unfortunately, being lost as brick houses take the place of the traditional mud homesteads. The individual designs of each ethnic group and even each family can be seen in this practice. A decorated house is the sign that the family follows, respects and nurtures traditions and conserves cultural values.

The Ndebele Mapoch Village to the north of Pretoria is built around a central quadrangle, with brightly painted houses under large shady trees, each surrounded by a painted seat where the villagers can congregate. The houses are decorated with geometric patterning that includes stylised contemporary objects, such as street lights and aeroplanes. The Ndebele wall patterns have been widely publicised and are seen copied onto museum and craft-shop walls, T-shirts and even a BMW. Nyathela Mahlangu is a wall painter from Kwaggafontein, who recently took her daughter, Zodwa, to the United States to assist her in painting the walls at Evergreen College in Washington State.

OPPOSITE PAGE:
Ndebele painted wall.

THIS PAGE, FROM TOP:
Basotho Cultural Village. Brightly painted wall; Early Ndebele painted wall and finial.

personal adornment

While visiting one of the Phumani paper-making projects in Winterveldt to the north-west of Pretoria, a group of young men – all dressed for the final ceremony of their initiation – came walking towards us. We admired their beadwork, which was very elaborate and used many different sizes and colours of bead as well as feathers and other found objects. We asked who had made their finery and, almost unanimously, they told us it was the work of their grandmothers.

The desire to decorate the body and accessorise clothes crosses all social boundaries. Sometimes, the adornment is to set oneself apart from others and sometimes it is a symbol of belonging to a specific community or event.

Beadwork is made and worn throughout the country and is a major component of traditional and ceremonial dress. The beads were finely stitched onto the cloth or blanket in broad bands, worked into the weaving of fabrics or sewn onto animal skins. They were a sign of social rank or status and acted as protection for the wearer. In times gone by, glass beads were produced from melted trade beads that had been cast in a mould and would be added to beads of natural materials.

The combinations of materials and ingenious techniques such as the woven patterning under the hats of Zulu women or the beaded embroidery on the *nceca*, worn over the shoulders of the Tsonga women, are examples of this originality. Xhosa and Ndebele beaded cloaks are almost too heavy to be worn, but exhibit fine craftsmanship and creative ability. The women of Venda wear *mwembe*, made in two parts from bright striped cloth stitched with braid, one part tied around the waist and the other worn over the shoulder. The outfit is completed with a corded neckpiece finished with a daisy-like tassel at the nape of the neck.

Beads were originally made from such materials as seed pods, bone, semiprecious stones, seashells and other found materials. These were eventually replaced by or complemented with bright glass beads introduced by Arab and Phoenician traders from Venice, Egypt and Rome, and have today largely been replaced by finely manufactured Bohemian and Czechoslovakian beads.

collectors

There was a time in the history of South Africa when craft objects were not generally appreciated, but museums and collectors have played a very important role in their conservation and popularisation. Craft has become an integral part of the lives of Helen de Leeuw, Kim Sacks and Karel Nel, and they, in turn, have shared their knowledge with many people. The commitment by these individuals – among many others – to promote, conserve and record the craft of South Africa is a fine example of the contribution made by collectors to the local industry.

OPPOSITE PAGE:
Traditional bowls with chair. (Collection: Karel Nel).

THIS PAGE, CLOCKWISE FROM TOP LEFT:
Jabu Nala. Terracotta beer pots. (Kim Sacks Gallery);
Pedi headpiece. Beads, cloth, metal, plastic found objects. (Collection: Kim Sacks); **Kim Sacks**. Vessel. 'Recent conversations with my ancient continent'. Porcelain, thrown and altered, sagger-fired.

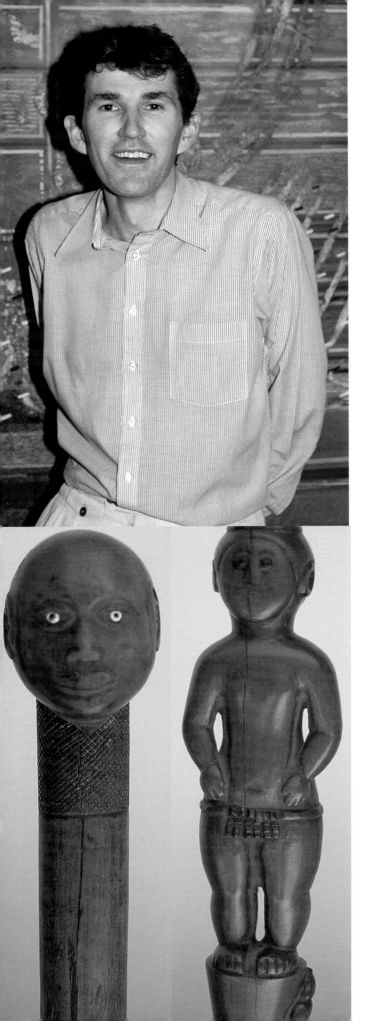

Karel Nel

Karel Nel bought his first crafted object as a 10-year-old boy. He feels that, through objects made by hand – craft objects, one broadens the understanding of mankind and his sensibilities. As a writer constantly expands his or her vocabulary in order to express the depth of knowledge, so too a collector of craft increases his understanding of mankind and life through the aesthetic appreciation and contact with each object in a collection. Karel is one of South Africa's most committed craft and art collectors and conservationists. It is because of this commitment that many of the collections and individual objects that had left South Africa have been returned to their rightful place.

Karel is a professor of Fine Art at the University of the Witwatersrand, where he lectures for six months of the year. He travels for the other half of the year, following his interest in art and its links to science and spirituality. His extra-large paintings of the Marquesas Islands exhibit these combined interests and his quest for an understanding of man's place on earth and in the universe.

When Karel asked about the meaning of 'art' in Venda, he was told: 'Art is any object of beauty made by hand with considerable care.' Karel agrees with this philosophy and reveres the objects with which he comes into contact. A pair of antique ivory arm bangles, simply cut from the tusk of an elephant and yellowed with age, are wrapped in dark blue velvet, and there are many other such objects in Karel's care, stored in deep shelved cupboards in his home.

Karel's house is designed as a series of vaulted rooms that open into the garden at one end and onto the large, square dark pool in the central courtyard at the other. The minimal display of selected objects in his home is chosen with the complete knowledge of his collection, the connection between the objects themselves, their history and use, the making process and material, and from where it came. All are relevant to his calm and uncomplicated way of living.

THIS PAGE, CLOCKWISE FROM TOP:
Karel Nel; Zulu walking stick; Xhosa walking stick.
(Collection: Karel Nel)

Helen de Leeuw

elen de Leeuw opened the Craftsman's Market, the first shop in the country to exhibit and sell the craft of Africa alongside contemporary designer furniture and modern homeware, in the early 1960s. The tumbleweed became her logo and a symbol of both her design integrity and her commitment to craft.

Soon after the end of World War II, Helen left a lecturing post at the University of the Witwatersrand and, with her very young daughter, Marike, went to London to do her PhD in English on Virginia Woolf. Helen remembers that she was unhappy, cold, broke and lonely in London, but was accepted as a part-time student at Camberwell Art School, where she learnt to throw pots. She returned to South Africa a potter, but without a PhD – something she has never regretted.

On board the ship on which she travelled home, Helen held a successful exhibition of her 'London pots' and, soon after her return, curated an exhibition entitled *Design for Living* in a large department store in downtown Johannesburg. On exhibit were works by Cecil Skotnes, lino cuts from the Polly Street Art Centre and mohair weaving by Coral Stephens. This innovative exhibition was a great success and it was not long after that she opened the Craftsman's Market in the basement of the same building.

Over the years, Helen opened other shops – the largest in Hyde Park, Johannesburg – and introduced craft and good contemporary design into many homes and to many people searching for local craft objects. There was always an interesting exhibition in a space reserved for craftspeople to exhibit and sell their wares – sometimes the work of local craftspeople and sometimes others, such as Bernard Leach, who exhibited pottery from St Ives.

Today, Helen de Leeuw lives in Glencairn in the Cape with her daughter Marike and her family. Her creative influence has been passed on to her daughter and granddaughter, who is a jewellery student showing the talent and eye for design inherited from her grandmother.

THIS PAGE:
Helen de Leeuw.

Kim Sacks

Kim Sacks has created a world of her own through craft. At her renowned gallery in Johannesburg, she sells the craftwork of many of South Africa's best-known artists. The gallery is a fusion of architectural styles taken from her travels all over the world and combined into a statement on Africa. The entrance to the gallery is enormously high, with pots on the windowsills way above the entrance and the walls covered with the latest finds, displayed in layers of time, colour and object. Although the outside of the building is painted a rich terracotta, the interior is bright jewel colours, which show off the natural tones of many of the objects to their full potential. Wooden stools and low beds from Central Africa set off the rows of telephone-wire baskets and shelves, packed with beaded animals and other whimsical objects, while traditional terracotta pots sit comfortably next to the work of contemporary potters.

Her world of craft has its roots in her home, which is filled with all the objects she loves and has collected over a lifetime of travel and intense interest in people, traditions and their craft. Some items are very old and valuable, while others she collected simply because they are unusual or zany. There are pleated goatskin *isidwaba*, or Zulu skirts, with exceptional beadwork yokes, Tsonga skirts with beaded fringes, *nceca* with animal imagery, Zulu hats, a wonderful pink headdress and belt beaded with Smartie-sized bright plastic baubles. She says she has created her own planet, which is both comfortable and personal.

After much ceramic experience and travels through Europe, Sacks arrived at the Royal Danish School of Art in Copenhagen, where she studied until her return to Johannesburg to open a teaching studio. She still makes fine porcelain pots, runs the studio and the gallery, in addition to caring for her two daughters and clock-making husband.

OPPOSITE PAGE:
Kim Sacks with her daughters, Maia and Tali.

THIS PAGE, FROM LEFT:
Kim Sacks Gallery. Entrance; **Kim Sacks**. Porcelain vessels decorated with plastic-coated wire, woven by **Joseph Msomi**.

exhibitions and craft

by Rayda Becker
Curator of Artwork – Parliament

The exhibition is a medium. None of the other more commonly recognised media, such as films, newspapers, articles or television, deal with objects in the same way. Exhibitions use real, physical objects, such as paintings, baskets and photographs, and not reproductions of these. Although all media deal with experience and response, the fact that exhibitions display the real thing allows for a different kind of reaction. The physical presence of the object, its scale, technique, colour and tactility (although 'do not touch' signs pervade many exhibitions) are present for the spectator to see and react to directly, and the response is filtered through the spectator's experiences and knowledge.

However, in the same way as other media, the exhibition involves interpretation and narrative, although here the curator is the author. As with other media, the exhibition involves a process that starts with conception, moves through selection procedures and ends with realisation. The curator, like the author, choreographer or director, remains responsible for the choices, arrangements and interpretation. Most exhibitions take place in spaces dedicated to this activity – a gallery. In short, exhibitions are relationships between objects, curators and spaces woven together by concept and interpretation.

Craft objects possess the same physicality and tactility as other objects and exhibitions that deal with craft and, it can be argued, are essentially no different from any other. Taking this point further and using one craft type, such as a basket as an example – you could substitute a finely engraved pot, beaded doll, hand-printed textile or any other familiar craft object –

imagine the differences between the experience of seeing a finely woven basket and a reproduction or text about it. Imagine the basket in a display (or visit an exhibition) and consider the approach and manner in which the work is displayed and how this can add to an understanding of it. If displayed in an exhibition examining grass weaving from ancient times to the present, the basket can be a historical object and form part of a development; if part of a display where the object is isolated and spot-lit, the basket can be viewed primarily as an aesthetic object. It could form part of an exhibition dealing with techniques, where you could admire the basket for its fine woven texture and perhaps compare it to another woven from plastic bags or rougher fibres; or imagine it in an exhibition dealing with local knowledge, where the basket could be displayed as a unit in a system of measurement, or a storage container for ritual items made in a particular shape or marked in some significant way. Baskets can be used in exhibitions examining gender, or used to exemplify the differences between art and artefact or craft.

OPPOSITE PAGE, FROM LEFT:
Baskets from the Northern Province made by Tsonga women, from the exhibition titled *Motho ke motho ka batho* 'People are people because of other people' held at Pietersburg Museum (The Irish House). The arrangement of baskets, from small to large, shows that each is a unit in a system of measurement; **Johannes Segogelo**. Carved wooden and painted soccer players. *'Soccer is Power!'* Popular Culture in South Africa Exhibition at the University of the Witwatersrand, Gertrude Posel Gallery.

THIS PAGE:
Venda drums or *ngoma*. *Art and Craft Heritage Exhibition*. Pietersburg Museum (The Irish House).

Imagine an exhibition that shows the development of baskets from old to new. Initially, the shape of these shallow baskets remained unchanged but, with the shift in the medium from grass to telephone wire, a number of inventions occurred in new weaving techniques, designs, imagery and colour, and these led to important new markets and new functions. It is interesting to know that traditional *izimbenge* are still made for use by local Zulu communities. The tradition continues alongside these new forms. Such changes are evident in many other crafts as well – such as walking sticks and beadwork on cloth – and such an exhibition would conceptually be underpinned by notions of change and development. Imagine, too, another kind of display, where the basket was not presented as special or part of history, but simply placed in a pile for sale.

All these imagined exhibitions show that there are many different styles and strategies for displaying craft. There are as many possibilities as the object itself can suggest and curators with the ideas and the spaces to hold them. They also reveal how the meaning of an object (the basket) can shift or be emphasised through exhibition. These displays also make the point that all objects, even a simple basket, carry multiple meanings and interpretations.

It is also through the exhibition that objects can be resuscitated and reinterpreted and, it can also be argued, that the current interest in craft is the result of such exposure. In other words, it is through public presentation, the medium of the exhibition, that craft is now receiving the attention it deserves.

In the same way that the history of modern art can be told through exhibitions, so the changes in evaluating craft can be told through exhibitions. It began with the exhibition *ART/artefact* curated by Susan Vogel in 1988 at the African Art Museum, Washington, in the United States. This was a show that dealt with the history of display. But, at another level, this exhibition – in its consideration of the migration of objects (those previously considered artefact or craft) from ethnology museums to art galleries – spoke of the accompanying changes from value to knowledge. And it is that which continues to inform us, as curators, in our thinking about the exhibition of craft.

conclusion

Through the continued exposure of craft exhibitions, in museums, in homes and the work place, many more people will become acquainted with the traditions and context of craft and aware of its importance to the culture and heritage of the country. If craft can be put in context among the numerous objects that surround us all and given the respect and consideration it is due, the patina of the old, well-used objects will add warmth and familiarity to many private and public spaces in the future.

OPPOSITE PAGE:
Interior design by Wilson and Associates, South Africa, Intercontinental, Airport Hotel, Johannesburg. (Photograph by Frances Janisch, NY)

THIS PAGE, FROM TOP:
Exterior walls on Ndebele homestead; Interior of house in Basotho Cultural Village with clay walls, pots and baskets.

transitional

Clive Sithole – from the BAT (Bartel Arts Trust) Centre in
Durban – is an excellent example of a transitional
craftsperson making work using the traditional skills and
raw materials of the rural potter, but whose work shows a new
idiom of one-of-a-kind craft objects sold through galleries and up-
market shops.

Clive learnt pottery as a child in Soweto, but when he moved
to Durban he saw the wonderful black, spherical pots made by
Nesta Nala and decided he would like to learn her pottery
techniques as she had skills she had learned from her mother that
were not accessible to everyone. Clive worked with Nesta for
some time and then went to work with Rebecca Matibe in Venda
to study her use of terracotta clay and graphite. Ian Garrett, who
had also worked with Nesta while studying for his Masters Degree
at the University of Natal, taught Clive his method of burnishing
the surface of the clay to give a natural lustre. Today, Clive makes
large, burnished terracotta pots that incorporate all these
traditions into his own individual work.

The strings of bright red lucky beans joined by a filigree silver
clasp created by Kubendrie Asim Kumar, a jewellery student at
Natal Technikon, show the combination of traditional silversmithing skills and new materials. Kubendrie focuses mainly on an
Indian-African aesthetic when designing her jewellery, so she

THIS PAGE, FROM TOP:
Kubendrie Asim Kumar. Necklace. Silver and 'lucky bean' seeds from the tree *Erythrina acanthocarpa* These seeds are thought to be a charm against evil; Necklace. Silver and pearls.

uses seeds, garnets, amethysts or colourful glass beads from Africa, strung together with silver links from a more conventional jewellery tradition. This allows her to create a wide range of culturally rich jewellery.

In both these examples, the new products are made for the contemporary market by craftspeople who realise they have the ability to earn a living from their craft if the boundaries of tradition are widened.

A wealth of craftspeople all over the country still use the skills of their forefathers, but experiment with different or new materials, be it plastic, telephone wire, found objects or any other that may have caught their imagination because of the colour or, maybe, because of the accessibility as they move away from the rural areas into the towns. On the other hand, craftspeople with access to traditional materials, such as wood, basket-weaving grasses and fibres, beads or clay, may begin to alter their product range to suit the market, whether it be the tourist or homeware markets, or even the field of high fashion. Very often, product developers are involved in this process because they have an intimate knowledge of markets and can assist with colour, style and design, as well as the quality and finish of the products, and can give guidance on production techniques and productivity. The importance of linking crafts to tradition and the culture of the country is vital as it gives relevance and a sense of place to the craft, ensuring that a South African 'style' will continue to evolve.

After her first visit to South Africa, Janet Mansfield, editor of the Australian magazines *Ceramic – Art & Perception* and *Ceramics – Technical*, said of the craft she had seen:

> *It was a pleasure and a privilege for me to travel in South Africa. Ceramics – Art now speaks in an international language, with its practitioners addressing contemporary and global issues. In South Africa, this is also the case; the numbers are strong and the quality equal to world standards. I found there is another dimension to the South African expression in all its crafts and art, that is, no doubt, a result of the landscape and the culture. These factors result in a unique style that is distinctly its own.*

Sometimes, craftspeople work alone, but frequently a group of people come together to work on a project. The participants need not necessarily be craftspeople, but should have the ability to learn tactile skills. The growing tourist industry and expanding markets in the craft field present a unique opportunity for the product base to grow and for the employment in the craft industry as a whole to increase, bringing sustainable income to disadvantaged people in many corners of the country.

THIS PAGE, FROM TOP:
Michelle Legg. Burnished terracotta vessel with a reference to old lace; **Jabu Nene**. Black slip stoneware bowls with sgraffito stripes.

pot making

The archetypal African aesthetic of rounded pots with a burnished clay surface, sometimes subtly patterned and sometimes smoothed and left unembellished, is of considerable appeal to potters as well as to collectors and decorators. The warmth of the colour and the satisfying form are the inspiration in many craftspeople's work. Among these are Simon Msilo, Ian Garrett, Michelle Legg and Lynnley Watson as well as Clive Sithole. They all work in terracotta clay, making large rounded pots by hand, which they burnish to a high gloss and fire either in a traditional pit kiln or in a simulation of one. The pots are not made for utilitarian use, but are decorative objects altered by changes in form or the surface decoration.

Simon was one of the earliest members of the Katlehong Art Centre, to the east of Johannesburg, where he still works and teaches his skills to young potters. Simon alters the neck of his pots and adds raised designs to the surface. Ian Garrett is now working with a fine clay slip or *terra sigillata* that gives a subtle polished surface to his pots, which he marks with mussel shells in elegant arcade patterns. Ian still hand builds all his pots as he feels strongly that they symbolise the essence of living in South Africa. Michelle Legg uses similar pot-making techniques, although with an entirely different aesthetic. She is presently completing her Masters degree at the Technikon Witwatersrand, incorporating designs taken from old lace as the reference for her decorative treatment on the shoulders of her highly burnished pots in a fusion of African and European aesthetics.

OPPOSITE PAGE:

Unkown Potter. The bulbous clay pot was purchased in Limpopo from a vendor at the side of the road. (Photograph by Reto Guntli, Agi Simoes)

THIS PAGE, FROM TOP:

Michelle Legg. Burnished terracotta vessels; **Ian Garrett**. Coiled burnished vessel; **Lynnley Watson**. Highly burnished large round pots. Fired.

Other ceramists have also incorporated the patterns and symbols of Africa into their ceramic works. Because of the continuous reference to earth colours, slips or washes of coloured clay are used in preference to conventional glazes. Some of the many craftspeople using these techniques are Henriette Ngako, who hand builds round pot forms that have developed and become sculptural, mythical creatures painted with coloured slips, and Jabu Nene, who carves geometric patterns into the dark slips he paints onto perfectly rounded, thrown, stoneware bowls. Jabu glazes the interior with a bright glaze to complement the matte exterior. The pots made at Rorke's Drift are decorated with *amasumpa* or added pellets on the surface, as are Nesta Nala's pots, and completed with wonderful blue and brown slip brushwork. Many other ceramists refer to Africa in their work through the material, the landscape and the flora and fauna of the country.

Large garden pots are very popular, mainly because of the love of outdoor living and the opportunity to grow a variety of plants because of the excellent weather. Indigenous plants are particularly suited to the rough terracotta clays and matte

earth tones. Dina Prinsloo makes site-specific pots designed specifically for particular plant species. Collen Kapa coils meticulously formed garden pots for the design shop Bright House, while Andrew l'Estrange coils very big, rough terracotta pots that are incorporated into garden landscapes.

Digby Hoets and David Schlapobersky make large stoneware pots, fired in high-temperature fuel kilns, reminiscent of Eastern storage jars. Esias Bosch brought the traditions of high-temperature reduction firing from Britain, where he studied in the mid-fifties at the height of the excitement over oriental techniques and the resurgence of studio crafts. There are many ceramists who follow the philosophy of 'truth to material' as it is well suited to rural potteries and the craftsman's way of life.

THIS PAGE, FROM LEFT:
Dina Prinsloo. Sculptured terracotta pot;
Decorated chair and terracotta Venda pots.

OPPOSITE PAGE, FROM LEFT:
Dina Prinsloo. Pots and sculptures; **Collen
Kapa**. Garden planters for Bright House.

basket
weaving

Crossing the suspension bridge over the river to see what new and fanciful animals have been made from telephone wire by the Telkom group on Skeepersdal farm – in the Muden area of northern KwaZulu-Natal – is always worth the adventure, according to Frieda le Grange. Over the past few years, Telkom has been funding a project to bring the process of telephone-wire weaving to communities throughout the country. Elliot Mkhise – said to be the innovator of the telephone-wire basket – gave the initial skills workshops but, since then, they have concentrated on a different style of basket from those found in Durban, as well as in- and out-trays for the office and some charming wire creatures.

After the training, the group returned to the farm and began knotting and twisting the wire to see what possibilities there were to make new and exciting artefacts. Mfanafuthi Ngubane makes wonderful creatures, including small black-and-white porcupines. Frieda does the marketing with the assistance of Agnes Mavuso, who attends the craft fairs and festivals to sell the wares of the entire group.

OPPOSITE PAGE, FROM TOP:
Agnes Mavuso. Ucingo Project. Telephone wire baskets;
Mfanafuthi Ngubane. Porcupine. Telephone wire.

THIS PAGE, FROM TOP:
Mfanafuthi Ngubane. Zebra. Ucingo Project. Telephone wire; **Mfanafuthi Ngubane**. Bird with orange beak. Ucingo Project. Telephone wire.

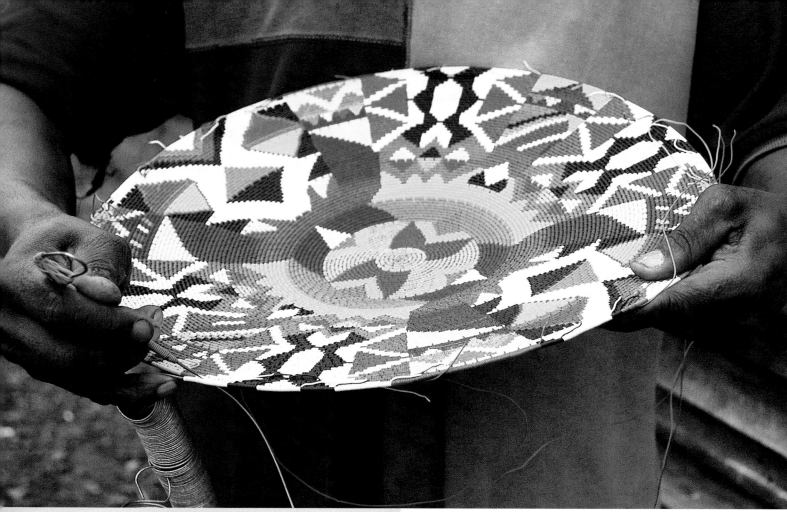

The creativity exhibited in the design and execution of telephone-wire baskets seems to be inexhaustible. Wire products have been made in southern Africa for many hundreds of years, and then, when technology was introduced and the colourful plastic-coated copper wire that makes up telephone cables was introduced, it proved to be irresistible to craftspeople. The wire was probably first used by Zulu night-watchmen to decorate their sticks, but has spread widely since then. Basket makers incorporated this new material into their repertoire and found the patterns of the coiled bright colours intriguing. Those basket makers with pattern-weaving skills found freedom to be creative with figuration and combinations of bright colour. Some of the baskets have layers of interwoven design and imagery, creating huge flat basket forms that are quite remarkable.

Elliot Mkhise grew up in a family of craftspeople and learned to make baskets as a child. After watching night-watchmen decorate their sticks with the colourful telephone

wire, he began weaving with it, using the basket-making techniques he knew so well. He has taught many others the skill and still makes wonderful baskets himself.

Ntombifuthi Magwasa, who won an FNB Vita Craft Award for one of her outstanding telephone-wire creations, lives in the Siyanda informal settlement outside Durban and although she has no formal training, has a natural sense of colour and design that has made her one of many very gifted wire-basket makers in the region. The BAT Centre has become a nucleus for telephone-wire baskets and assists craftspeople with training, materials and marketing possibilities. Alice Gcaba, working from her small home in Siyanda, weaves small houses and domestic scenes into her baskets, and Vincent Sithole has images of butterflies, bees and flowers woven into his. There are many other wire-basket makers, too numerous to mention by name, in and around Durban, all making outstanding products using innovative and individual patterning.

CLOCKWISE, FROM TOP LEFT:
Elliot Ndwandwe. Working on telephone-wire basket in Siyanda; **Ntombifuthi Magwasa**. Telephone wire basket. Detail. (1998 FNB Vita Craft Now Exhibition Winner); **Alice Gcaba**. Telephone-wire baskets; **Elliot Mkhize**. Wire basket; **Vincent Sithole**. Telephone-wire basket. Detail.

mdukatshani

Mdukatshani – meaning 'The place of lost grasses' – was a badly eroded labour farm with few prospects when Neil and Creina Alcock moved there and Creina began a beadwork project with the women of the region. The veterans and Creina have been together for 27 years now, although she feels that craft was 'always a part-time activity, even when it was a full-time job'. Today, the grass has re-grown, and the beadwork and copper-wire eggs and bowls have transformed the lives of hundreds of people.

Tessa Katzenellembogen came to the region in the late 1980s, and began teaching a destitute group of flood survivors to make baskets out of scrap telephone wire. Using need rather than skill as the criteria for the selection of craftspeople, small sparks of hope were kindled and these would later develop into the exquisite and innovative wirework that continues today under Creina's leadership. The wire products provide a steady source of income for craftspeople in the Waayhoek Resettlement Village, the Nhlawe Land Reform Area, and the Mdukatshani tribal area in the Tugela basin in central KwaZulu-Natal, where the decorative tradition continues to flourish. It is one of the last places in KwaZulu-Natal where you can still see women wearing tribal dress, with ochre headdresses, pleated leather skirts, and wire bangles and anklets.

Because of the legal restrictions on telephone wire at that time, craftspeople began experimenting with fine-gauge industrial copper wire, developing a range of woven copper articles, often interwoven with beads, that include eggs, bracelets, napkin rings, jewellery and baskets, all exquisitely finished and highly decorative. Some of the objects, such as the eggs and bangles, have become bestsellers and can be found in craft shops all over the country, and are the financial mainstay of the groups that make them.

The copper-wire baskets have had less exposure for the simple reason that they are far slower to make, taking up to two months to complete a single basket. These are, however, now becoming a popular range of wares, as the soft sheen of the copper wire when formed into a small rounded basket or a large fruit bowl is irresistible to decorators and homeowners. Although many of the first beaders, spectacles perched on their noses, are still at work, a new generation is starting to dominate, ensuring the long-term continuity of the project.

Everyone at Mdukatshani has his or her own story of hardship that has brought them here. Both Ngakhelaphi Mkhize and Elias Mtshengu, who started the project with Tessa, are still there. Ngakhelaphi Mkhize (Ma Mkhize) was one of the original pupils and now teaches copper-wire craft to other group members. She demands a high quality from her pupils as she is a perfectionist who works at a slow, contemplative pace and refuses to be rushed.

While Elias Mtshengu won first prize in the copper section at the *Contemporary Zulu Basketry Exhibition* in Johannesburg in November 2000 – he gave his prize money to his son, Thamasanqa, so that he could complete his matric – Ma Mkhize was a bronze award winner. Her early work set her apart from others in the group and, although she always had different skills in which she took great pride, she preferred to work in copper. She has passed her care and craftsmanship to her eldest daughter, Gwinya, who is a star copper-egg maker.

Elias Mtshengu grew up poor and an orphan, who left school at an early age and started working with copper. Now both his wife and a son, Thamasanqa, have joined the basket-making groups.

OPPOSITE PAGE, FROM LEFT:
Beadworkers at Mdukatshani in tribal dress; **Sizani Mbatha**. Mdukatshani;

THIS PAGE, FROM LEFT:
Elias Mtshengu, Mdukatshani. Woven open copper bowl or *sungulu*; **Mgongo Ngubane**. Mdukatshani. Hand woven copper bowl or *khamba*. Copper wire, beads.

Orders were initially sporadic and there were long periods with no orders at all when, unexpectedly, an order from Paris set him busy on the large, coiled copper basket – known as a *sungulu* – that won him the prize in 2000. Since then, he has been working on orders for *sungulus*, but is still afraid that they will run out and he will once again be without work.

Sizani Mbatha started working with beads when she was in a prison cell – as a 90-day detainee under a proclamation intended to curb violence. After a historic legal battle, she was however released just before the 90 days expired. Although the police had agreed to let Sizani work on beads as a pastime, as soon as she was released she returned to her 'real' job of building dams with stone and cement. She has completed 41 small dams – and has also excelled at all the other tasks she has undertaken since she joined the Mdukatshani development project 26 years ago. She has led teams of children on soil reclamation and gardening projects, helped to fence kilometres of bushy hills, dug boulders out of stony land for fields, and completed many other tasks.

Sizani returned to beads a few years ago when funds for a poverty relief scheme failed to materialise, and she realised there was little chance of making a living off the land. She applied herself to learning to make copper eggs and then graduated to woven copper baskets.

Hardship has made her resilient, and she is known as a fighter. Versatile, headstrong, intelligent and determined, Sizani is a perfectionist 'with the mind of a man'.

These are just some of the stories behind the craftspeople whose decorative beaded eggs and large open copper bowls can be seen in the interiors of homes from Johannesburg to Paris.

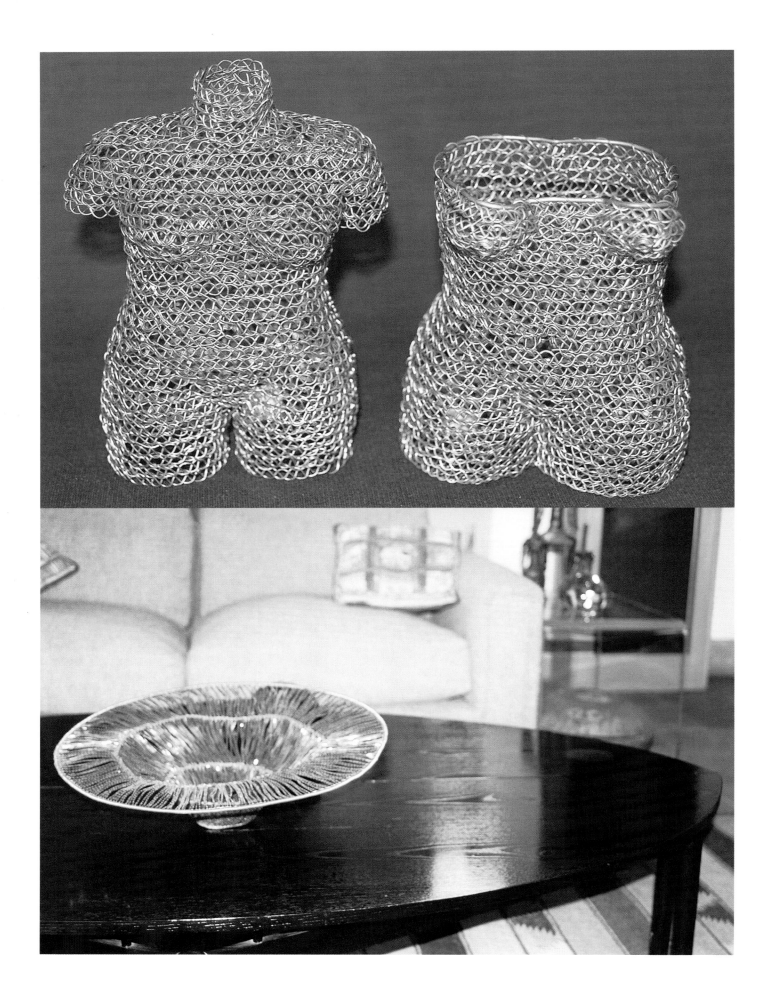

The link with a tradition of decorative wirework goes back almost 1000 years, and there are several Early Iron Age sites at Mdukatshani, evidence of a culture obsessed with the use of metal. Walter Oltmann notes that 'although very little information is available on the early manufacture of wire in South Africa, it is likely that wire was made indigenously as early as the first millennium AD'. This was essentially a Central and southern African craft, and traditionally the preserve of men. Walter Oltmann, one of the finest artists in the country, uses this craft technique to form his giant insect sculptures and screens. This use of craft techniques by fine artists is an interesting facet and once again brings the discussion of the division between art and craft to the fore. In this situation, it is almost certainly the intent of the maker that decides the positioning of the final piece.

Weaving new forms is not the prerogative of the wire-basket makers. Using the skills and natural materials of basket making, new forms and contemporary coloured stains, such as mauves, purples, ochres and cerise, basket makers are keeping up with modern trends and have cornered their share of the market. There are beautiful baskets of fine ilala palm coming from the Lubombo Spatial Development Initiative in the far north of KwaZulu-Natal, where the traditional shallow bowl is now made in soft pastel colours or bright vibrant tones and the finely woven 'carrying' baskets are sometimes finished with a natural wooden handle. Flat, patterned baskets from the North-West Province or the highly decorative baskets from Eshowe are frequently seen grouped on the walls of kitchens and garden rooms as the soft natural tones add warmth and texture to the space. The *imbenge*, or beer-pot covers, all individual in design and surface treatment, are also seen grouped on walls or as a focus on a chest or tabletop.

OPPOSITE PAGE, FROM TOP:
Lindelani Ngwenya. Copper-wire torsos; **Zodwa Duma**. Copper-wire and glass-bead bowls. (Collection: Audrey Coleman)

THIS PAGE, CLOCKWISE FROM LEFT:
Zodwa Duma. Copper-wire and glass-bead bowls. Zodwa was trained at Mdukatshani, but now works in Johannesburg where she has trained a group of women to make bowls similar to the ones she makes; **Lubombo Spatial Development Initiative**. Bowls and detail of a woven basket.

THIS PAGE, FROM LEFT:
Woman wearing traditional Venda costume;
Woman wearing traditional Tsonga *nceca*.

cloth decorating

Decorated fabrics are still used as daily attire by a large number of women throughout South Africa. They are tied around the shoulders or worn as a skirt, headscarf or cloak, used for tying a baby onto the mother's back or spread on the ground to sit on. It is these traditional cloths that have caught the eye of decorators and collectors, and have given craftspeople the opportunity to extend the uses of fabric in many ways. Often, they are patterned with beadwork depicting everyday images, such as dogs and houses, or embroidered with brightly coloured thread. Many new products, such as cushion covers, bags, tablemats, scarves and wall hangings, are being made using these techniques.

THIS PAGE:

IFA. The CSIR (Council for Scientific and Industrial Research) Project in Venda uses traditional cloths that are embroidered and decorated with beads, and made into cloths, cushions and bags.

mapula and karosswerkers embroidery groups

Co-operatives from Winterveldt and Letsitele

'Goodbye Hands and Knees, Hallo Electrolux' is embroidered across the middle of a brightly coloured wall hanging by Selina Makwana. There is an image of a 1950s housewife in a neat little apron, proudly using her new vacuum cleaner, and other images of domesticity. Two versions of the cloth were made; one was bought by Electrolux for their head office, where it hangs in pride of place, and one hangs in the Art Faculty office at the Technikon Witwatersrand.

Selina comments: 'Jannetjie van der Merwe helps with the selling of the embroideries. She found us in the land of hunger, but now the money we get from the embroideries pays for household products and school fees. After my cloth won the prize at the 1998 *FNB Vita Craft Now Exhibition* held in Cape Town, many people rejoiced.' There was yet another reason to rejoice when the innovative Mapula group won the Gold Award at the 2000 *FNB Vita Craft Now Exhibition*.

Mapula – meaning 'mother of rain' – is a project in Winterveldt, a semirural area about 45 kilometres north of Pretoria. It was started about 10 years ago as a collaborative effort between the women of Winterveldt, the Sisters of Mercy in the region and a group from Soroptomists International.

Initially, all embroidery work took place at the mission but, for the last few years, half the women have been

THIS PAGE AND OPPOSITE:
Mapula Embroidery Group. Black fabric, embroidery threads. 2000 *FNB Vita Craft Now Exhibition* winners.

embroidering on their own, and delivering their completed works to Rossinah Maepa, a group coordinator. Usually, one person does the embroidery, but occasionally there is collaboration on larger works or commissions.

More than 80 needleworkers belong to Mapula, earning a living from creating colourful embroidered work. Rossinah was invited to take embroideries to the *Celebrate South Africa* exhibition in London in 2001, and her comment on her return to South Africa was: 'It was the first trip but not the last. I believe I will fly again. I am proud of the Mapula project because it changed my poor life to a better one.' Her dream is to build a house for herself and her family and to be able to give her children an education – a dream that is fast becoming a reality for Rossinah and her co-workers in the Mapula project. In its early stages, members of Mapula embroidered cushion covers and calico shirts, but the embroidered cloths and wall hangings have proved to be especially successful and have provided the embroiderers with the widest scope for innovation. The designs are drawn onto the fabric in crayon, sometimes with the assistance of Rossinah or her daughter, or one of the other women with

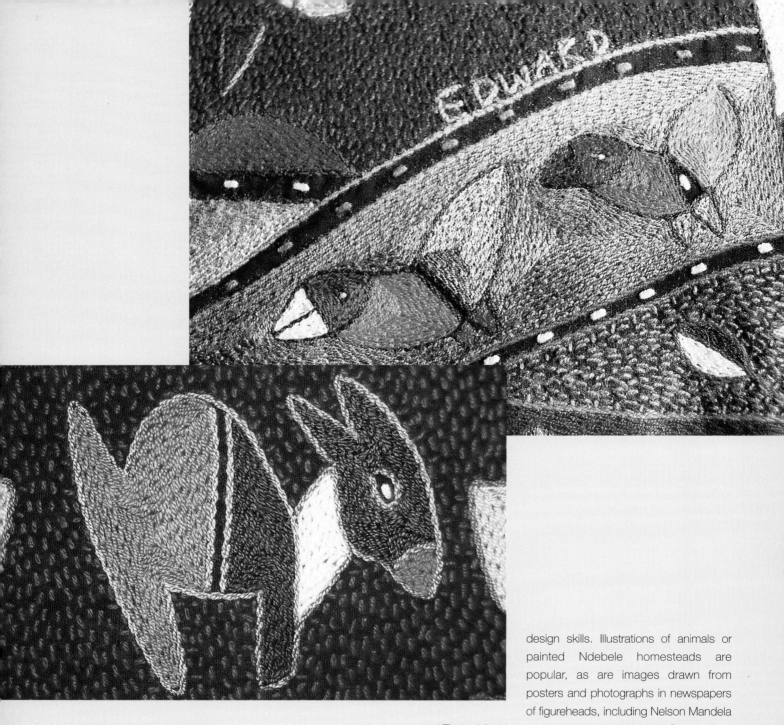

EDWARD

design skills. Illustrations of animals or painted Ndebele homesteads are popular, as are images drawn from posters and photographs in newspapers of figureheads, including Nelson Mandela and Thabo Mbeki, or sportsmen and entertainers. Some cloths are embroidered with signs from the Arrive Alive safe-driving campaign or posters from the AIDS education programmes.

Karosswerkers is an equally dynamic embroidery project in Letsitele, close to Tzaneen in the Limpopo Province, and has undergone shifts from the imagery it used when it began. In the early years, Irma van Rooyen, who began the project, designed the embroideries with a geometric border surrounding a central field of stylised animals or foliage. Later, Solomon Mohati began to execute some of the drawings, incorporating forms found on local craft objects, and now Kelvin Machlawaule has

joined the group and uses references to oral histories or scenes from contemporary life on the cloths.

The Karosswerkers project began in 1988 on the orange farm Irma and her husband had purchased. Initially, five women joined the project, but it has since grown to about 600 people – a huge enterprise that includes participants from surrounding farms as well as villages and settlements up to 100 kilometres away. Among the many talented women is Flora Ngobeni who, won an FNB Vita Craft Award in 2000 for her embroidery.

The drawings are prepared on cloths and embroidery threads are supplied to the embroiderers. When the cloths are complete, the women bring them to the centre to be hemmed and sewn into cushion covers, mats and wall hangings.

OPPOSITE PAGE:
Traditional cloth or *nceca*. Details. Textile, beads, mirror, wool and safety pins.

THIS PAGE, FROM TOP:
N'wa-Mitwa Mania. Tsonga woman making metal jewellery in Polokwane.

The unusual combination of beads and safety pins in circles around small round mirrors is used to pattern the traditional *nceca*, which is worn tied over the shoulder by Tsonga women in the northern provinces of South Africa. Some of these works are now sold in galleries and have become collectors' pieces, but many are still worn by the makers. The floral cotton tablecloth used for the beaded *nceca* is decorated with a new creative patterning executed over the original floral of the cloth. The result is enormously rich and colourful and, when combined with other cloths and brightly coloured turbans, is a most decorative garment. Some of these patterns have been incorporated into a unique range of cushion covers, runners and vibrant scarves by Matiti Magic. Through the intervention of the Council for Scientific and Industrial Research (CSIR), traditional craft skills are being turned into highly marketable products in local markets.

In mid-2001, an exhibition entitled *The Melting Pot* was curated by Dr Rayda Becker in Polokwane. The exhibition linked the traditional crafts of the Limpopo Province and the crafts of today. The proverb *Motho ka motho ka batho* – 'People are people because of other people' – was used to express this continuation of craft skills. The designer products were displayed in the museum alongside the traditional craft and, on the opening day, all the craft groups were present to sell their work. Sophisticated bags, shawls and cushions made from the vibrant red-and-turquoise striped fabrics, beaded and stitched to give a unique, rich finish, were brought from Venda; Tsonga metal bangles, to be worn on arms and legs, were rolled by the craftsperson who held the wire taught between her toes while rolling the bangle on a metal anvil using an impala horn. Traditionally, small rivet-like metal rings are also used to make Tsonga jewellery and now elegant, contemporary pendants are made using this material and the same technique. Block-printed cushion covers and

bags with traditional motifs lay alongside nappa-leather cushion covers, subtly altered by the addition of traditional metal beads of the Ngove people, and tassels made of hemp and leather for curtain tie-backs, plus many other products, including brightly beaded sneakers. The colourful *nceca* and the tightly pleated and beaded skirts worn by rural women attracted much interest, and curious city folk appeared to take great delight in discovering their own traditions in the museum.

The inventive patterning of the !Xu and Khwe – KhoiSan people now settled in the Northern Cape – has been translated into a range of fabrics using printing, dyeing and painting techniques. The group started by making lino cuts of their well-developed, traditional patterns and imagery, which are a source of great pride and empowerment to the community. Under the guidance of Cheryl Rumbak, a range of eight basic designs was developed and transferred onto screens in preparation for fabric printing. A wonderful array of backpacks, dressing gowns and other household items are made from these fabrics, which are sold in their Cape Town outlet, Kamatoka, at the Montebello Craft and Design Centre.

Traditionally, the !Xu were artists and carvers, while the Khwe – originally from Angola – were mostly basket weavers. Their ancestors are best known for their rock paintings depicting narratives of daily ritual and complex mythology. Today, the !Xu and Khwe work with a wide range of materials, making prints, wooden artefacts, ceramics, baskets woven from grass and recycled plastic, hand-worked tin frames, as well as their well-known jewellery made from leather and beads crafted from ostrich eggshells.

A similar fabric-printing project has been developed in the Richtersveld to the far west of the Northern Cape. The Nama women of the region developed images for silk-screening onto fabric, using the unique plants and trees of the area as their reference. These women also make ceramics planters, which are filled with some of these extraordinary plants.

THIS PAGE, FROM TOP:
Ngove Nappa. Nappa-leather cushions incorporating handmade metal beads; **Ngove Nappa**. Curtain tie-back with nappa leather and handmade beads.

OPPOSITE PAGE:
!Xu & Khwe. Bowl made from recycled plastic and orange bags on block printed fabric.

the mobile craft school

One of the biggest problems facing craftspeople is the distances that must be travelled to attend workshops or to get their product to markets and stores. To overcome this problem, Mpumalanga Province has developed a Mobile Craft School in an eight-ton freight carrier, custom built to fold out into 160 square metres of covered space. With a three-phase generator, this carrier will allow rural craftspeople access to a state-of-the-art IT system that will connect them immediately to local and international markets via the Internet. It also includes a studio that can accommodate 20 individuals at a time, and is equipped for training programmes in woodwork, sewing, printing techniques, jewellery design, beadwork, painting and drawing, ceramics, papermaking, industrial design, as well as wire and metalwork. An on-board up-to-date library containing magazines, journals, books and videos in the field of décor, design, fashion and style allows for the development of products in line with global trends. An aesthetically pleasing and effective exhibition system ensures that the latest work from the mobile unit, or exhibitions from other projects and centres, can be displayed for local communities to see.

beadwork

by Fiona Rankin-Smith and Julia Charlton

Beadwork has always been an important part of South African culture. Although it is not yet known when beadwork first emerged, illustrations from as early as the mid-1850s show people wearing beads.

Beaded items of adornment and clothing denote identity and status. This is particularly the case among women, who are generally both the makers and wearers of beadwork across South Africa's many language groups. Beadwork styles and their meanings are passed down from one generation to the next, as an extension of oral traditions and the shaping of traditional value systems. The forms and their connotations are both fluid and powerful. Beadwork also conveys wealth and importance, and a person wearing a particular item may be identified as an important member of society.

The use of traditional items of beadwork in contemporary contexts can have powerful sociopolitical implications. The most famous example in recent history occurred on the day of Nelson Mandela's sentencing during the Rivonia Treason Trial, when he chose to signal

CLOCKWISE, FROM LEFT:
Makosha messages. Framed bead circles on fabric produced in the Makosha Village, Limpopo; **Pedi** apron. Cloth, beads, plastic, found objects. (Collection: Kim Sacks); **Lindafrika**. Beaded cushions.

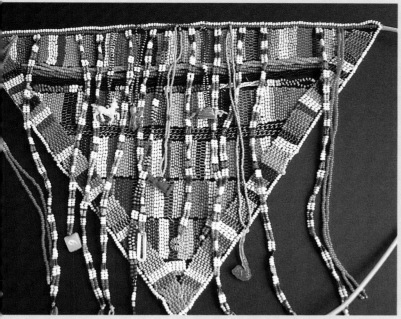

his rejection of apartheid's judicial system by wearing traditional Eastern Cape clothing, including a Tembu beaded-collar necklace. Nowadays, the wearing of beads on occasions such as the Opening of Parliament has become commonplace, as proud celebration of South Africa's cultural diversity.

Many contemporary musicians and designers include beadwork and beaded clothing in their wardrobes, which communicate an idea of African heritage across different cultures without necessarily denoting a specific ethnic grouping. Pop star Brenda Fassie, for example, sometimes wears traditional Zulu attire, and sometimes more generic forms of beadwork. Ringo, the Eastern Cape singer, performs in semi-traditional waistcoats that appeal to a nationwide audience, and fashion designer Marianne Fassler, whose clothing is directed mainly at a white market, uses elements from traditional South African beadwork as reference material.

Growing international interest has prompted a number of collaborations between beadworkers and designers in the development of contemporary products with an African feel for sophisticated foreign markets. The resulting objects, such as cushion covers, pyjamas, bedspreads and necklaces, for example, are sold in a variety of different outlets, such as fashion houses and design stores, and their proliferation testifies to the fact that beadwork is part of an evolving tradition that is always changing and never frozen.

Fashion-conscious Londoners were entranced by the elegant garments shown at the *Celebrate South Africa* exhibition in 2001. Zodwa Mahlangu, from Kwaggafontein in KwaNdebele, designed a two-piece evening gown for the exhibition using the Ndebele traditional beaded 'bridal veil' in brightly coloured patterns falling from a beaded bodice. The chic, striking garments sold very successfully in London.

Zodwa lives with her parents and older sister in a beautiful painted traditional homestead, where she works with colleagues making beaded dolls and covering ostrich eggs and wine-glass stems with beadwork. She also makes a range of evening bags worthy of international markets.

Zodwa realised her young friends were not interested in their own traditions, so she started a dance group to attract them and, from there, slowly lured them into making beadwork. Today, they all work from home, producing individually designed articles, which Zodwa collects and markets for them.

There are many crafts groups working with beads all over the country, but it is most common to find beadwork based on Ndebele, Zulu or Xhosa traditions. By highlighting the varying techniques, designs and colour choices from Zodwa's Ndebele background, Jane Bedford's Zulu group and the work of Ndeleke Qangule, who is Xhosa, these strong traditions provide fine comparative examples of transitional beadwork.

Ndeleke Qangule grew up in a rural environment and was exposed to beadwork and other crafts throughout her childhood. Her mother was a schoolteacher in KwaSaki, Middledrift, between King Williamstown and Alice in the Eastern Cape. This community embraced their 'tribal' way of life, which included beadwork, song and dance. So, between school and holidays spent with her family in the Transkei, Ndeleke enjoyed the contact with the people of KwaSaki – young and old – as there was always something new to learn. Ndeleke worked as a senior nurse until she retired to work with the craft groups and to follow her interest in the traditions of her Xhosa heritage. She has won numerous awards including that of Ma Afrika in 1999 – for the preservation of traditional art and crafts.

Ndeleke is the coordinator of Nomakwezi Craft Centre – meaning 'morning star' – and Nomachile Skills Development Centre in Port Elizabeth. These programmes were set up to research traditional Eastern Cape Xhosa beadwork and needlework so as to revive and conserve the traditional skills.

The groups base their production range on the traditional Xhosa use of fine black braid and stitching onto cream, ochre or bright red cloth, accented with small mother-of-pearl buttons and black, white and turquoise beads, which is ideal for bags, bedspreads and stylish waistcoats and skirts.

THIS PAGE:
Zodwa Mahlangu and dolls outside her home near Kwaggafontein, KwaNdebele.

OPPOSITE PAGE, FROM LEFT:
Ndeleke Qangule. Bag with beads and buttons, and dancing stick; **Jane Bedford**. Beaded necklaces.

The members of the craft centres are taught relevant skills so that they can set up independent units or groups, which are encouraged to develop their own personal expression and individual range of products. The groups have had some unusual commissions since they started. They were, for example, asked to make beaded items for traditional doctors and their assistants. The design for these items had to be accurate in every way as they reflect the status and the specialty of healing of each doctor. The choice of colour is prescribed in a dream or by the spirits – who work through the healers. Another interesting project was to research and design beaded, symbolic garments for Basotho families to be worn when they welcomed home their initiates from the mountains. In contrast, they also make company logos and promotional items, jewellery, and homeware products. The Port Elizabeth Museum and the CSIR commissioned them to reproduce selected artefacts, such as an elaborate 'dancing stick' and beaded, long-stemmed pipes made from indigenous wood for the museum collection.

Jane Bedford has designed a range of rope-like necklaces based on a traditional Zulu pattern symbolising beer flowing through a basketwork sieve. Each section of the necklace varies in colour from the next, and the necklaces of different lengths are also subtly varied in colour. The effect is dazzling and sophisticated. The revival and production of this particular technique is being passed on to the children who assist their mothers when they get back from school, but now even the men and boys want to learn, so the women are holding workshops to teach them.

Jane has been working with beads for 18 years and now has over 80 Zulu women working in the project. Every two weeks, a small group of the women come to her house to learn about product development and to learn the techniques or new colour combinations required for the range in production. When the beadworkers leave to go home to work with their groups, they are given beads, the final designs and orders that have to be fulfilled. Two weeks later, they return with the products – all of excellent quality and according to specifications.

The range of beaded work they produce includes jewellery, cutlery handles, animals, bags and many other items. Delicate beaded flowers were originally designed and woven by the women specifically for a competition, but these have now been included in the production range. They are an outstanding example of the creativity and skill of the designers and beaders in the KwaZulu-Natal region.

Traditional dolls or fertility figures have enjoyed renewed interest since the remarkable exhibition *Evocations of the Child* was launched in Johannesburg and toured the country in 1998. Dolls in an abstract form are used for education, ritual and initiation throughout South Africa, and they are carefully made according to tradition, reflecting the differences in culture-specific beadwork. Today, many craft groups make a simplified form of these traditional dolls, and these are then sold commercially to the tourist and collector markets.

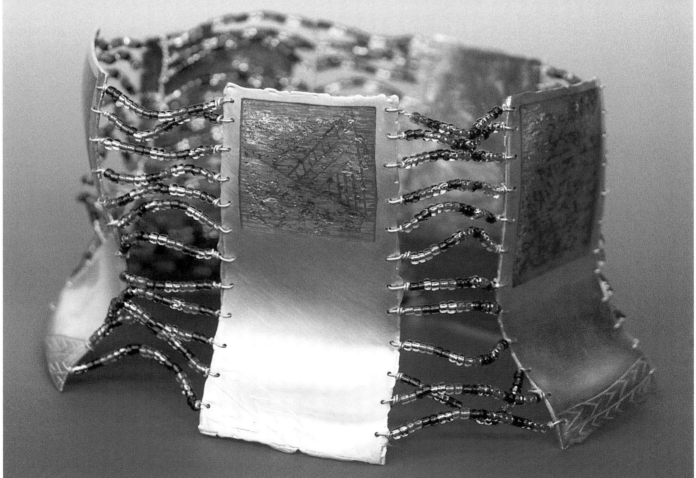

jewellery making

Much jewellery is made in South Africa, both in formal institutions that have the facilities to teach traditional techniques such as gold- and silversmithing and the informal sector, which encourages individual creativity and the use of found and recycled materials. Beverley Price uses images cut from magazines and comic books set in tin to make new ornaments based on traditional jewellery forms, such as the Ndebele bridal apron or the Zulu love letter. Geraldine Fenn uses combinations of found objects, perspex and words torn from magazines to make wearable objects. She also uses handmade glass beads and silver in her work.

Jewellery design schools and individual teachers have set a process of change in motion, and creative, innovative jewellery – using everything from metal and precious stones to recycled tins and paper – are being made throughout the country.

Brightly coloured, beaded, safety-pin necklaces and bangles and even bridal tiaras, baskets full of rainbow-coloured telephone-wire bangles alongside subtle, lustrous, copper-wire and bead bangles, are all available in craft shops and jewellery stores. The range of bead necklaces and earrings, traditional love letters, bottle-top necklaces, rolled paper beads, wire and seeds, traditional KhoiSan ostrich-eggshell beads and PVC pipe – carved to look like ivory – are all produced by craft groups and individuals working in this field.

The impetus that attracts jewellers to use these non-formal materials and creative images is partly driven by jewellery lecturers promoting the concept of a new aesthetic in South Africa. If this creativity and innovation can be harnessed to drive the jewellery industry, there will surely be a new wave of jewellery, free from its association with wealth and status.

OPPOSITE PAGE, FROM TOP:
Beverley Price. Neckpiece. Recycled cable wheel, found objects, niobium, elasticised thread; **Beverley Price**. *Mapungubwe transfused*. Silver, vitreous enamel, 24-carat gold, glass beads.

THIS PAGE, FROM TOP:
Geraldine Fenn. Neckpiece. Silver, plastic bug. Detail; **Geraldine Fenn**. Bracelet. Handmade glass beads with silver details, silver chain. **Geraldine Fenn**. Sterling silver rings.

transitional jewellery

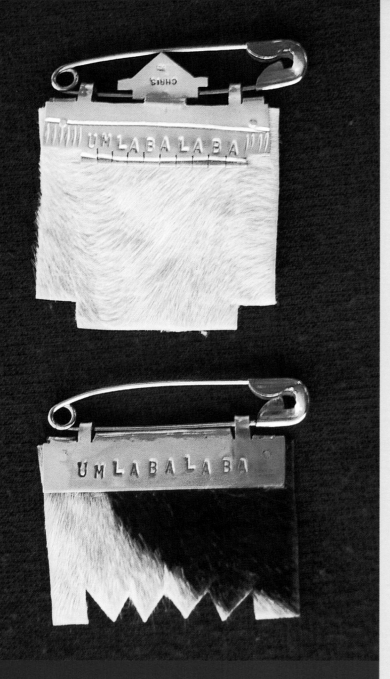

by Chris de Beer
Jewellery Department, Durban Technikon

What I have been looking for is a new type of jewellery – the type that is similar to picking up a shell or pretty stone or leaf when going for a walk – so I've been exploring the decorative quality of jewel-like objects. This coincides with my work at the Technikon, where we prepare students for the market but they all seem to avoid the commercial jewellery in search of something else. In recent years, the realisation that Italy makes more money from our gold than we do has prompted the jewellery industry to think about starting the search for an indigenous form of jewellery that is still fragmented and uncoordinated.

Because of my own exploration and interactions with the Zulu students in my department, and the need to understand them and to unlock the potential if there is any, I have started to identify opportunities that could lead to the development of an indigenous body of jewellery. One of my students, in particular, alerted me to the possible existence of a Zulu sensibility that could be tapped into. His name is Sonwaba Alvan Mthethwa. Sonwaba made what I considered to be the first indigenous pieces of jewellery by a Zulu student. Unfortunately, he was killed in a motor accident in 2001.

THIS PAGE FROM TOP:

Chris de Beer. Bracelets. Top: *'Sitandwa sami'*, the Zulu words for 'Love of mine', made for Valentine's Day; Others tell of loyalty and love. Recycled motor-car number plates with words stamped on aluminium strips; **Chris de Beer**. Brooches. *'Umlabalaba'*, the Zulu name for a popular board game. In these pieces, *umlabalaba* refers to the political games people play. Safety pins, cow hide, words stamped onto strips of sterling silver.

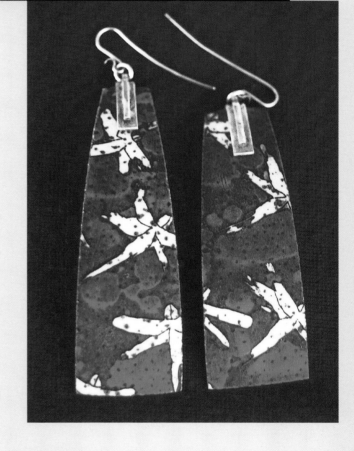

Being in Durban, I am exposed to various types of craft, such as basketry, beadwork, traditional Zulu dress and woodcarving. I have recognised these skills as a possible approach to establishing a new type of jewellery. So, when I was approached to teach a jewellery skills course for Zulu craftsmen, I jumped at the opportunity. After teaching them basic jewellery skills, they produced quite interesting pieces, but not really anything that hinted at the establishment of a new genre. I realised that one should probably base one's search on existing indigenous skills, with only minimal jeweller's interference. This is how the woven ilala bangles with metal strips came into being. These were the result of a community project done under the auspices of the Lubombo Spatial Development Initiative in conjunction with the African Art Centre. I began by teaching a group of 30 people, mostly women, basic jewellery skills. The brief was to include skills training and recycling in the programme. After the first training session, I realised that we needed to base our work on an existing craft, so we called on Thembe Nkanini from the KwaJobe area, who assisted with the training. We soon discovered that most of the women already knew how to weave these bangles, so we showed them how to cut cold-drink cans into strips and to incorporate them into the bangles. Feedback led us to substitute the cold-drink cans for recycled litho plate, which seems to have resulted in improved quality. Now all that needs to be done is to market these bangles.

I do think that one of the ways forward for the jewellery industry is to identify the skills that are available and to explore ways of developing them into jewellery forms. The designers are being trained at various technikons around the country. The educators should simply focus on these possibilities and make it part of the syllabus.

THIS PAGE, CLOCKWISE FROM LEFT:
Lubombo Spatial Development Initiative, in conjunction with the African Art Centre. Bracelets woven from ilala palms and recycled litho plates found in scrap yards; **Marlene de Beer.** *Isikhumba* (meaning skin or hide) bracelets. Sterling silver, rivets, cow hide; **Chris de Beer** Earrings. Ostrich eggshell, sterling silver, etched with hydroflouric acid, oil paint.

woodworking

Bheki Myeni describes himself as having 'camera eyes'. Since childhood, he has lived near the Umfolozi Game Reserve in KwaZulu-Natal, and has observed and recorded the herds of wild animals that roam in the reserve in his small carved animals. As a child, he started carving animals and insects from the wood of indigenous thorn trees. His work is usually quite small and, because the wood is soft, he can carve finely and fast, completing an animal in about two hours. His animals have a unique character, individual and animated, as if they may move if touched. The cheetah lies down and scratches its back or drinks from the river, the hyena rolls in the mud, and the jackal waits, ears alert.

Bheki burns the details of the animal into the wood in the traditional Zulu manner, but instead of the usual poker, he uses pieces of broken car bumpers. Many of the other woodcarvers also use this technique – the wooden meat platters and butter dishes from the Lubombo project are accented with darkened coin-spots and stripes while Sibosiso Maphumelo carves angels wearing 'burnt on' dark glasses, 'as a sign that they can see into our hearts and our minds without our having to speak.'

Bheki is currently teaching carving skills at the local school. His youngest child is interested in drawing and his wife sometimes assists him with the carving, especially the giraffes, which she says are easy for her as she has watched how he does it for many years and now feels competent to help him. Bheki is a modest man who loves his work, but he is not afraid to approach shops and galleries, and is proud that he is able to make enough money to support his family.

Alson Zuma makes two-dimensional wooden panels and friezes carved with animals. He then uses the burning technique together with dyes or polish to darken the image. For the *FNB Vita Craft Now Exhibition* in 2000, he made a chest decorated with symbols and messages using this technique and then installed a radio and tape recorder inside it. This piece, entitled *Radio Alson*, won a merit award. The comic carvings on the chest depict the various topics he talks about on the news tape – music, finance, soaps, medicine, agriculture, the weather and traffic reports.

OPPOSITE PAGE, FROM TOP:
Sibosiso Maphumelo. Carved wooden angels with sunglasses. Details burnt into wood. **Bheki Myeni**. Carved wooden animals. Spots or other details burnt into the wood.

THIS PAGE:
Peter Schutz. *Madonna of the Revealing Heart*. Jelutong wood, oil colours. (Collection: Lucia Burger)

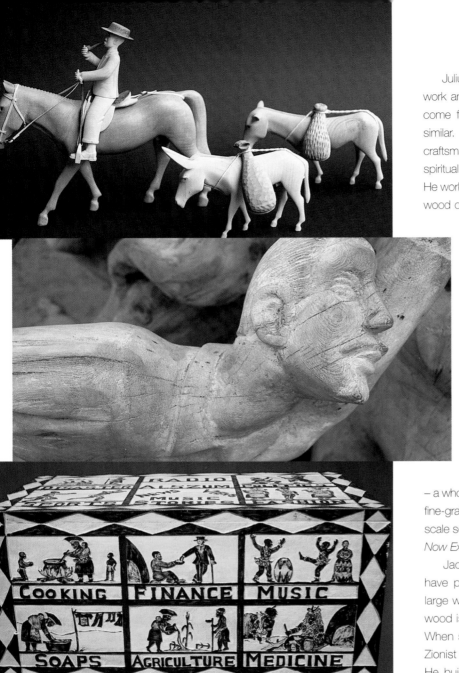

Julius Mfethe and Peter Schutz both carve great detail into their work and finish the surface to a silky smoothness. Although they come from diverse backgrounds, their technique and scale are similar. Peter comes from a European tradition based on fine craftsmanship and finely carved images, mainly of a sacred or spiritual nature, often addressing the conflict between good and evil. He works in small parts, such as a head or a heart carved from hard wood or red ivory, which can be worked on while in the kitchen or any other place. When complete, the parts are assembled into larger sculptures of angels and saints, and then sealed and brightly painted. A few years back, Peter made a series of landscape chairs, incorporating images into the structures but is presently working on angel-like figures depicting the constellations of the southern hemisphere.

Julius started carving images selected from his environment using just one simple pocketknife. He was born near Port St Johns in the Transkei and, as a 12-year-old, carved goats from pieces of white stinkwood, which he sold to a trader for 50 cents each. Over the years, he realised he had a keen eye and a photographic memory, and this has enabled him to expand the range of subjects he carves to include images he sees in magazines or newspapers. Julius still works mainly with white stinkwood – a whole tree provides wood for about six months – but uses other fine-grained woods for contrasts and intricate detail on his small-scale sculptures. In 1997, Julius won first prize in the *FNB Vita Craft Now Exhibition* for his carving.

Jackson Hlungwani and Noria Mabasa are craftspeople who have pushed the boundaries of their creativity and made very large wooden sculptural images. Both come from Venda, where wood is plentiful and there are many creative people in the area. When still a young man, Jackson was ordained into the African Zionist Church and, from there, created his own religious group. He built a stone palace to the glory of God and carved huge wooden figures and large fish as icons and symbols for his New Jerusalem. Jackson also carved bowls and flat serving dishes to be used in traditional manner in the homestead. Jackson used the bowl, which is the centre of social sharing in the African community and from which everyone eats, as the symbolism in his enormous, carved *Bowl for Nations*.

Noria worked in clay until she experienced a series of ongoing creative dreams inspiring her to carve from large trees washed down by a flooding river. She had seen the process and the subject matter in her dream and was not daunted by the size of her sculptures. The images of crocodiles, snakes, domestic animals and people locked in combat exhibit her vision of images hidden in the natural materials.

THIS PAGE, FROM TOP:
Julius Mfethe. Farmer and donkeys. Carved white stinkwood; **Noria Mabasa**. Detail on wooden 'drum' sculpture; **Alson Zuma**. *Radio Alson*. Carved wooden box with radio and tape recorder, in which Alson records his news and views of life at Fort Nottingham.

OPPOSITE PAGE:
Jackson Hlungwani. Portrait.

product development

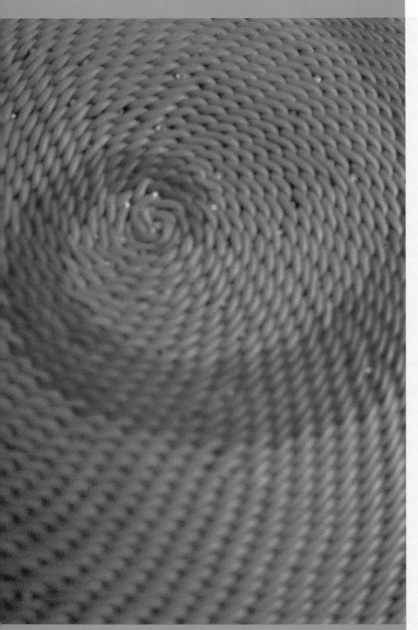

Product development or product design is the conscious planning of the appearance, making and the function of a product based on the traditional skills and craft products of the particular community. As Dr Ben Ngubane, Minister of Arts and Culture said in his speech at the launch of *Design Indaba 2002*:

> *This has worked very well in the craft sector, where we were able to demonstrate successfully that design is able to lift a traditional object that has existed for many years to new aesthetic levels.*

Product designer Tamar Mason feels that South African craftspeople are masters of innovation when it comes to product development:

> *... perhaps because we are at the crossroads of so many influences – the developed and developing world, Western, Eastern and traditional African beliefs and languages, urban and rural communities, black [and] white people and everything in between. Our society is a real mixed masala, which can be great news for crafts. When product development does not happen, we see items being sold at flea markets and alongside the road, which have not changed for the last 30 or more years. This stagnation of design should not be encouraged, as many South Africans are quite happy to take risks to change their product.*

THIS PAGE AND OPPOSITE:
BAT Centre. Telephone-wire baskets.
Zen Zulu range.

Tamar goes on to comment that:

> ... *Product development excels when it comes to recycling. The waste of the industrialised world is looked at afresh by crafters and turned into desirable items. Little boys on dusty village roads and township streets delight in making themselves wire cars that often put engineers to shame. These early skills have been refined into developing galvanised wirework items that range from saxophone sculptures to fruit bowls and cosmetic shelves. Today, industry is being co-opted by the craft world and now orders wire display stands from the wireworkers.*

Marisa Fick-Jordaan made the leap from fashion designer to craft product developer in 1995 when she founded the BAT Shop, located on the edge of Durban's busy harbour. Her passion for transitional craft forms inspired her to develop an extraordinary telephone-wire basket range in collaboration with women from the Siyande informal settlement and, more recently, the Zen Zulu range, which fuses traditional craft skills with cutting-edge design.

These products have been snapped up by international and local home décor stores and galleries. The range is continuously updated with new designs and colours and has become a South African design classic.

The Cape Craft & Design Institute was recently established in the Western Cape to provide support to individual entrepreneurs and small businesses in the craft and hand-manufacturing sector. The Institute identifies specific products that could be developed within the educational programme of the institution, in conjunction with craftspeople and product developers – some for further commercial development and some as products for specific events and projects.

The Council for Scientific and Industrial Research (CSIR) is also working to increase the productivity of craftspeople and to supply the market with innovative South African products of high quality, using traditional craft skills or referring to the traditional craft objects to develop a new range of designer wares.

With these individuals and institutions – and many others besides – focusing on the design of craft products, a unique 'South African Style' will become a reality.

conclusion

Craft has become a means of job creation as well as an artistic outlet for many people and has proved that there are untapped skills waiting to be accessed all over the country. Craft has changed from a misunderstood, rather minor art form into one of the most publicised and important showcases of the heritage of South Africa.

OPPOSITE PAGE:
Ostrich Eggs in a recessed light cove create a contemporary light fitting. Design concept by David Muirhead of Wilson & Associates, South Africa. (Photograph by Frances Janisch, NY)

contemporary

OPPOSITE PAGE:
Susan Sellschop: Tree vessels and bowl, porcelain paper clay; Elias Mtshengu, Mdukatshani, Copper-wire basket or *sungulu*.

THIS PAGE:
Michael Methven, Paper-and-wire sculptures, Spier Wine Estate.

A small herd of gemsbok grazing in a field is not an unusual sight in southern Africa, but when they are made of paper and light up at night, they are worth stopping for. Michael Methven creates life-size sculptures of animals using the wire as a 'line drawing' that he covers in white paper and lights from within, giving an ethereal effect. He also makes 'hunting trophies' as wall lights and vultures that lurk on fences.

'Contemporary' is the title chosen for this chapter on crafts that have moved away from the traditional South African craft techniques and materials into the realm of design and production of unique craft objects. It is about a selection of craftspeople and designers chosen as examples of the diversity of creativity and technique, and as proof of the excellence and excitement of craft in South Africa today. The roots of various traditions may be glimpsed in the diverse approaches of craftspeople making one-of-a-kind objects of small production ranges for sale in galleries, decorating stores and design shops. The intuitive creativity of these craftspeople has focused on an aesthetic that further extends the 'style' so important to the craft industry in this country.

The diversity of approach of these craftspeople is one of the defining factors. The innovation for the unique craft object is

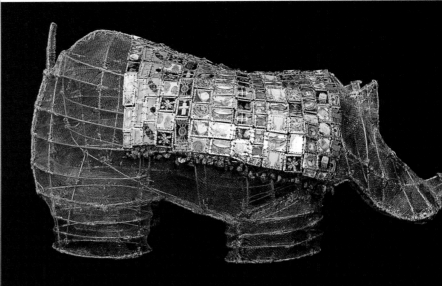

usually maker-led, whereas the design of small ranges of handmade craft is usually market-led, and the introduction of new materials is influential in increasing the product range. Resin, glass, paper, clay, wire, fibre and the many recycled materials are examples of this, while technology and manufacturing techniques, such as the use of moulds of many types suited to different materials, or commercial dyes, stains and colours now available, are but two examples. There is no limit to the creative possibilities and the combinations of materials and techniques in the craft arena. The potter, jeweller and weaver are all still working but have been joined by so many others using contemporary materials and techniques.

As *Time* Magazine recently stated in an essay on craftsmanship: 'what has most rekindled craftsmanship is the growing market for something distinctive in a world of sameness'.

THIS PAGE, CLOCKWISE FROM BOTTOM LEFT:
Donald Kubjana. Christmas tree. Shredded tin cans;
Street Wires. Wire flamingo; **Beverley Price**. Rhino –
Mapungubwe Remined. Wire, aluminium, paper, plastic, aluminium foil, pyrite (fools' gold).

OPPOSITE PAGE:
Wendy Goldblatt. Porcelain bowls.

pot
making

Anthony Shapiro throwing production bowls and Katherine Glenday throwing fine porcelain one-off bowls exhibit the difference in intention of two expert ceramists.

Anthony manages a production studio for the manufacture of tableware and designer wares. His bowls are simple, open, well-thrown forms glazed in the colours of the season, whether suede, tan and charcoal grey or soft celadon greens and pastels. Because of their simplicity, they are suitable for the table or any other place in the home. His range of vases depends on form for impact and come in similar colours to the bowls. He has a team of throwers, glazers and kiln packers, who have worked with him since he began in 1997, so throwing became the obvious means of production.

Anthony consults regularly with his customers and follows local and international design trends so that he is able to keep one step ahead of the market. He has purposely kept the factory small and can thus change colour or form with ease and oversee all the processes. He feels that there is an aura to thrown pots that is important to his aesthetic, but now – for efficiency and speed – uses slip casting for some of the regular ranges.

Katherine Glenday works with porcelain because of the whiteness, delicacy and translucency necessary in her quest to bring colour, light, texture and form into closer

OPPOSITE PAGE:
Anthony Shapiro. Ceramic bowls.

THIS PAGE, FROM TOP:
Anthony Shapiro. Ceramic bowls.
Anthony Shapiro. Garden planters with aloe.

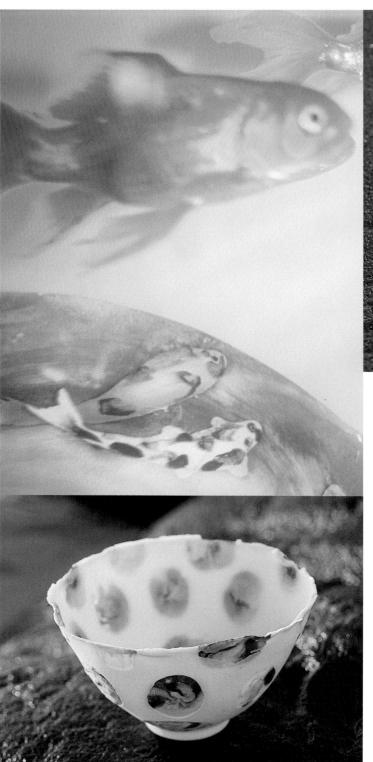

harmony. Recently, her work has become less to do with what is depicted on the surface but with the 'grain' of the material and what happens with the play of light through the walls of the vessel.

Another theme with which Katherine works is fish in pools or ponds. The challenge of depicting light shimmering through water and the sense of the movement of fish she sees in her dreams represent flashes of insight and inspiration, which she than paints onto her pots.

Katherine recently held a successful exhibition at the Irma Stern Museum, Cape Town, where she exhibited her fine porcelain bowls and containers grouped according to colour, on beds of shells, lentils and even coal. Some of the very thin bowls were exhibited in light boxes, which exaggerated the translucency and brought the surface to life. The dream-inspired fish bowls stood on top of a fish tank filled with large, warped and broken fish-decorated jars and shards of her work, together with bright orange koi fish swimming among them. Katherine feels that the effort and time spent on this elaborate display was time well spent. She says, 'The exhibition underlined for me that it is absolutely vital to display work in a worthy manner. The process spoke to me of the great continuum inherent in each of us, which links us with the creativity of the natural world'. The importance of relationships and relatedness was central to the themes of the works.

THIS PAGE, CLOCKWISE FROM LEFT:
Katherine Glenday. Porcelain vessel; **Katherine Glenday**. Shards of porcelain vessel depicting fish in water, which have been placed in fish tank with fish. Exhibition, Irma Stern Museum, University of Cape Town; **Katherine Glenday**. Porcelain vessel.

Potters and jewellers probably make up the largest group of craftspeople in the country. Both these crafts are taught at technikons and universities and have organised associations and regular exhibitions that bring the craftspeople together for discussions and exchanges of information. Perhaps this contributes to the popularity of these two craft forms.

There are a great many potters all over the country producing contemporary innovative work – both unique and production designer wares – for household use or interior design, as well as one-of-a-kind craft objects to be sold through galleries and exhibitions. To find the balance between these two avenues is often a hard choice for a craftsperson. Clementina van der Walt left a teaching career to set up a production line of brightly coloured tableware. She developed a decorating technique that was fast and effective and could be taught to others. The range has been extremely successful and is marketed internationally. Clementina has handed over the running of the factory to her partner so that she can return to making one-of-a-kind designer wares and creative vessels, with reference to historic ceramic styles as well as the South African landscape and culture.

THIS PAGE, FROM TOP:
Katherine Glenday. Porcelain vessel.
Katherine Glenday. Porcelain bowl on shells. Exhibition, Irma Stern Museum, University of Cape Town.

THIS PAGE, CLOCKWISE FROM BOTTOM:
Potter's Shop. Ceramic bowls on handpainted cloth;
Hylton Nel. Ceramic Cat; **Potter's Shop**. Decorated
ceramic bowls.

OPPOSITE PAGE:
Simon Msilo. Burnished sculptured vessel.

the production path

Clementina van der Walt
Maker of decorative ceramics

When embarking upon a career as an individual maker of handcrafted objects, the creator usually comes up against the problem of being unable to be fairly and lucratively remunerated for the time and labour invested in the object.

One of the ways to deal with this – and still remain in the field of creative making – is to turn to a broader production of objects, which entails employing people and streamlining the labour so that the manufacturing is more financially viable. The challenge is to maintain a sense of the quality of the handcrafted look so that the product does not compete with industrially produced items of the same kind. In addition, ideally, a balance needs to be maintained between the worldview entertained by a craft philosophy, and the practicalities required in the business world in terms of marketing, labour relations, client liaison and such. The former tends to focus on a 'from-the-heart' source, thereby generating a value system and lifestyle that may often be incompatible with the latter, where such esoteric values are not awarded the same priority.

THIS PAGE:
Clementina van der Walt. Handpainted ceramic plates.

The initiator of a production set-up could, however, view the entire enterprise as an opportunity to apply a holistic approach. This would be an attempt to view all the processes – designing, systems and techniques of manufacturing, staff training, business management skills, packaging, despatch, marketing, bookkeeping, public relations – as a means of communicating a sense of a deeper meaning of craft. The overall aim is to make utilitarian objects of excellence that reflect the spirit of the maker and the ethos of the times. To realise this goal requires a psychological and spiritual centredness on the part of the creator/production manufacturer. Although such qualities are, of course, most beneficial in any walk of life, the attainment thereof is more accessible via the path of the craft philosophy.

THIS PAGE, FROM TOP:
Clementina van der Walt. Handpainted ceramic cup.

The programmes taught at technikons prepare students for production of tableware and designer vessels and teach them, through a varied process, the social history of ceramics, as well as the technical and aesthetic skills required by a practising ceramist. Chris Smart, Samantha Brazer and Candice Feninianos were all trained at the Technikon Witwatersrand Ceramics Department, headed by Suzette Munnik.

Chris Smart produces a range of mugs, teapots and platters in varied colours. Besides the production line, he throws large vases and containers that are glazed in a lively green for a chain of hotels. Samantha Brazer makes leaf plates, flower-shaped bowls and other creative tableware. Her work reflects her interest in plants, insects and the reptile world. Her recent ceramic work is based on shells and the sea. Candice Feninianos makes brightly coloured tableware, but is best known for her large, ceramic melon slices for use as fruit bowls on contemporary tables.

Peter Mthombeni learnt about Technikon Witwatersrand when he telephoned a local newspaper to ask how to go about becoming an artist. This was in 1983, at the height of the apartheid era, when no black students were admitted. Notwithstanding, Peter set off for Pretoria to get ministerial approval to attend the Fine Art programme – and so began his art career.

Peter works alone or with an assistant, making a designer range of mocca and teacups, but is probably best known for his Ndebele and Zulu tea sets. These are designed to resemble a traditional village, with the homestead as the teapot and the sugar basin and milk jug as the entrance pillars. The teacups turned upside down become the smaller huts. These sets are meticulously made and decorated with traditional Ndebele patterning or to resemble Zulu beehive huts.

He began drawing when he was kept out of school for six months due to illness. He became so skilled and drew pictures of oxen that were cause for much envy at school that, with the encouragement of friends and a teacher, he decided to make art his career.

Peter's first year at the technikon was very difficult. He had little confidence and found it difficult to express himself, but everyone was helpful and friendly and he found that every student offered him something – a pen or an overall or paper, whatever was needed. He did well academically and won a prize in the annual New Signatures Competition. This earned him some status among the students and lecturers and he moved forward from there.

After Peter completed his printmaking diploma, Suzette Munnik and Clementina van der Walt – who were the lecturers at that time – persuaded him to enrol in the Ceramic Department to study for a second diploma. This launched him on his career as a ceramist. He was familiar with clay, as he had make oxen from the clay in a stream – as so many children had – and had fought battles with the *boereseuns* (farm boys), flicking clay *lats*, or pellets, as ammunition.

OPPOSITE PAGE, FROM TOP:
Chris Smart. Swan teapots. Ceramic; **Samantha Brazer**. Leaf platter with bee. Ceramic.

THIS PAGE:
Peter Mthombeni. Ndebele-inspired ceramic teaset. Gate posts are the milk jug and sugar basin, and the homestead is the teapot.

THIS PAGE, FROM LEFT:
Charmaine Haines. Ceramic figures. **The Potter's Shop**; **Chris Silverston**. Ceramic bowl and fabric.

OPPOSITE PAGE, CLOCKWISE FROM LEFT:
Karen Sinovich. Terracotta spoons glazed and decorated with images and messages; **Hylton Nel**. Hump-moulded plates with cat image.

Charmaine Haines lectures at Port Elizabeth Technikon with Mishak Musuku. Charmaine throws containers and vessels, which she alters by adding figurative elements to make sculptural vessels incorporating people and animals. Mishak is an excellent thrower, and when using imagery, moulds cattle in relief on his pots.

Ajanda Mji was one of Charmaine's students and was encouraged to develop her own symbolism. Since the untimely death of her sister and father, she uses angels as her influence on vases and candleholders. Ajanda also models the heads of birdlike creatures onto small bowls that are completed with small chicken-like feet. She has opened her own studio in New Brighton township in Port Elizabeth, the first township ceramic gallery in the country.

The predominantly casual lifestyle of South Africans and the appreciation of colour and the African reference means that many ceramists make tableware – mugs, plates, bowls, jugs, cups and saucers – all with individuality, to cater for this trend.

Karen Sinovich makes one-of-a-kind wares, Chris Silverston produces a small, individually decorated range and Clementina van der Walt creates a range of African-inspired tableware that has a huge international market. Karen's handmade teapots, spoons and containers – with whimsical quotes and messages written in bright colours on the surface

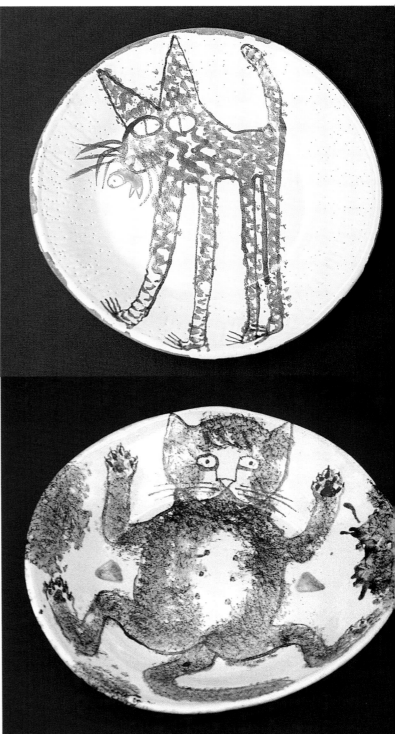

– illustrates the decorative, whimsical taste of the local market, as do the designs from The Potter's Shop in Cape Town, which are brightly patterned by a group of talented young men who work with Chris Silverston, the designer and owner of the studio.

Hylton Nel and Martha Zettler are two examples, among a great many, whose work is shown at exhibitions and in galleries both locally and internationally.

Hylton Nel lives in the small town of Bethuli in the Great Karoo and sells the main body of his work in London. He paints images of horses and cats and humorous portraits of his friends on hump-moulded plates and bowls. He also makes three-dimensional cats with mottled glazes – a quirky reference to English Staffordshire wares.

Martha Zettler was the winner of the Premier Award at the *Altech International Ceramics Exhibition* in 2000. She works in bone-china cast, which is then sandblasted and pierced. This process is extremely intricate as the sandblasting must be carefully controlled and the piercing precise as the pot can easily crack. The inside and raised portions on the exterior are glazed in white in contrast to the matte white of the body. The pieces are beautifully crafted and extremely delicate, and seem to float off the surface on which they are standing.

The Ardmore studios in the KwaZulu-Natal Midlands is a uniquely South African institution that has earned international acclaim for Fée Halsted-Berning, who began the operation in a stone outbuilding on their farm, and the artists who work with her. Bonnie Ntshalintshali, whose family lived on the farm, came to work with Fée in 1985. She had no art training and, in fact, hardly any formal schooling at all, but she had a natural feel for clay and for modelling three-dimensional objects and her sense of colour was immediate and vibrant. This partnership – sadly, Bonnie passed away a few years ago – was the core of a studio of artists from the area, working in a unique style developed through the years. Domestic ware, often on a grand scale, is coiled or thrown and then embellished with raised imagery. The reference for the decoration is taken from the plants, birds and animals of the area or from books of religious or mythological stories. The ceramics are brightly coloured and whimsical, and each object is created with care and an innovative spirit unique to the individual artists. Josephine Ghesa works at Ardmore, but makes individual sculptural pieces, her references coming largely from the myths of the mountains and from her dreams.

OPPOSITE PAGE:
Josephine Gheza. Three animal figurines. Sculpture. Painted and polished earthernware. Creatures are half-man, half-beast and hands form heads of other animals.

THIS PAGE CLOCKWISE FROM LEFT:
Ardmore. Detail of Zebra bowl; **Josephine Gheza**. Sculpture. Painted and polished earthenware; **Bonnie Ntshalintshali**. Detail of teapot. Carved and handpainted ceramic.

IZIMFENE NEZINYONI ZIHLEZI ESIHLAHLENI

CLOCKWISE, FROM LEFT:

Ardmore. Sculpture. Plate and bowl.

glass
making

The large pale turquoise glass flower-form vase at the entrance to the Kirstenbosch botanical gardens restaurant was made by Sue Meyer and Nelius Britz. They have found that they collaborate very comfortably on large architectural commissions as their design concepts are similar. They recently completed an installation of glass fish in the restaurant at the Arabella Country Estate hotel, which is close to the coast, so fish were an obvious choice, as was the use of nautical steel fittings for their suspension. Nelius's knowledge of the movement of schools of fish through water, gleaned from his deep-sea diving experience, proved to be very useful to the final imagery.

Both Sue and Nelius make individual glass objects as well. Sue uses *pâte de verre* in combination with fused glass to make colourful, sensitive containers and contemporary headrests based on the traditional forms. Nelius uses his past biological knowledge as the source of inspiration for his seasonal leaf forms cast in coloured glass. By coincidence, both were potters before they were seduced by the transparency of glass.

OPPOSITE PAGE:
Sue Meyer and **Nelius Britz**. Cast-glass vase. Kirstenbosch botanical gardens restaurant.

THIS PAGE, FROM TOP:
Sue Meyer. Cast-glass and *pâte de verre*. Sculpture.
Nelius Britz. *Thorns*. Kiln-cast glass.

Individual glass-blowers have been working and teaching from their studios for many years. The excellence of craftsmanship seen in the work of these craftspeople is witness to their innovation and skill. Glass was not commonly taught as a craft material in South Africa until fairly recently, when the Pretoria Technikon opened a Glass Design and Technology Department teaching both hot-glass techniques, which use molten glass, and cold-glass techniques, using kilns to slump and form the glass.

Retief van Wyk is the subject leader in the Glass Design and Technology Department. He prefers to work with cold-glass techniques, cutting and 'painting' with small chips of glass in very bright colours. When complete, the platter forms are fused and then slumped in the kiln. Retief has completed architectural installations, including windows in the Great Park Synagogue in Johannesburg, as well as domestic objects and trophies.

Nicolene Fourie makes opaque, cast-glass cones and discs in shades of green and blue with smooth, rounded, orange spikes on the surface. She combines these into sculptural forms, some top-like, others resembling sea-urchins or even a space ship. Nicolene uses *pâte de verre* made from recycled glass to make these colourful, creative objects. As a student at Pretoria Technikon, she found she did not enjoy glass-blowing, but preferred to use slip-cast ceramic moulds for her small but 'monumental' glass sculptures as the heat could be easily transferred and she had fewer breakages.

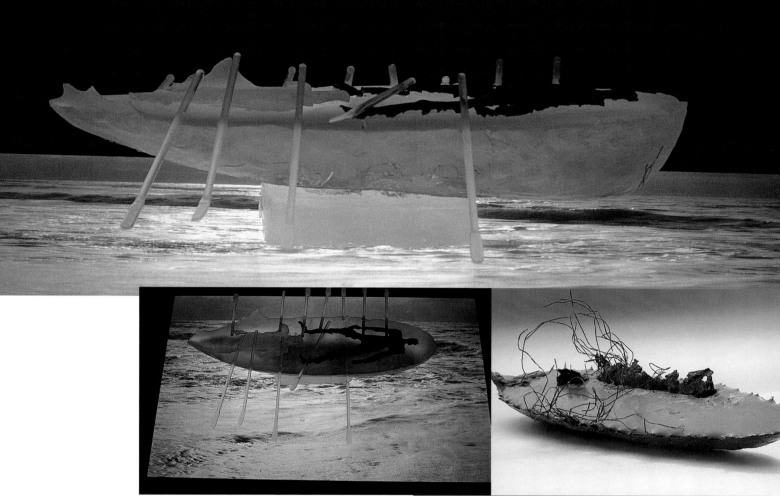

Iron ribs and rusty metal eroding from the surface of sand-cast glass boats, or found objects giving the impression of the sea and rock pools inside the boats, refer to the many rusty, slowly disintegrating wrecks that lie scattered up the Skeleton Coast of Namibia. Doreen Hemp uses the inherent qualities of glass – brittleness, fragility and transparency – to portray wreckage and survival. Her transparent glass boats allude to water, but what is sea and what is boat? Sometimes, she adds pieces of the wrecks themselves and displays the boats on large, photographic transparencies to exaggerate the translucency.

Rhé Wessels also assimilates water and boats into her glass images. She works with a combination of clay and glass – her two chosen materials, making vessels and sculptural forms using the translucency of the glass in contrast to the matte surface of the clay. The fine line between these fired and fluxed materials was addressed by Rhé in her Masters Diploma in Technology at the Technikon Witwatersrand.

THIS PAGE, TOP AND CENTRE:
Doreen Hemp. Glass shipwrecks. Sand-cast glass on light boxes with enlarged photographic transparencies.

BOTTOM RIGHT:
Rhé Wessels. *Retrospection. Pâte de verre* and ceramic.

jewellery

Contemporary jewellers are, yet again, often the product of formal training. The jewellery schools run by Stellenbosch University and Pretoria, Witwatersrand and Natal technikons all train students in the technical skills demanded by industry, but the innovation and final designs are the result of imaginative, creative jewellers.

Ronel Steyn and Errico Cassar both teach in the Jewellery Design Department at Stellenbosch University, better described as a creative workshop. Errico works with two design styles – baroque imagery in a contemporary idiom and the complete opposite, minimalist designs – while Ronel makes unusual, sophisticated jewellery in silver and gold, constantly exaggerating conventional proportion.

Lecturers and students work together to develop ideas and discover expressive techniques in tune with the trends in the contemporary design world. At the same time, they are sensitive to the historic roots and heritage of the traditions of jewellery production. The combination of the academic and the practical allows students the freedom to develop their own ideas and to prepare to set up their own studios.

Small silver containers with a cactus-like plant on the lid made by Jacqueline Lloyd are a link to sculpture, but allow for jewel-like detail. The boxes are small and can be held in the hand and examined – a quality found in Zulu snuff boxes. They become a jewellery-sculpture crossbreed that Jacqueline finds both interesting and challenging. The same qualities can be found in her 'seed pendants', which are also small boxes.

OPPOSITE PAGE:
Jacqueline Lloyd. 'Womb box'. Copper and enamel.
Jacqueline Lloyd. 'Tree box'. Copper and silver.

THIS PAGE, FROM TOP:
Ronel Steyn. Pendant. Silver; **Errico Cassar**. Brooch. Silver; **Errico Cassar**. Brooch. Gold. (Photographs by Mark van Coller)

THIS PAGE, CLOCKWISE FROM BOTTOM:
Ronel Steyn. Box brooch; **Jacqueline Lloyd**. *Walking with the shadow. Faith, suffering and redemption.* Copper bangle with hand signs; **Jacqueline Lloyd**. Seed necklace. Ebony, silver, 18-carat gold, enamel and rubber.

OPPOSITE PAGE:
Carol Potter. Brooch. Etched glass set in sterling silver.
Carol Potter. Brooch. Handmade glass bead, sterling silver.

'Scale is always an issue as I enjoy physical weightiness – exaggerated wonderfully in gold and platinum – but in jewellery that weight or volume can become uncomfortable or impractical to wear, so I found myself extending my work into decorative containers or boxes. I have also made occasional clocks, tables and functional-ware.'

Jacqueline Lloyd finds that the exhibitions of the work of diverse jewellers curated by Errico Cassar maintain and promote a culture of original and uncompromising design, which serves to keep the aesthetic skills of his past students up to the mark.

Carol Potter's glass beads, reminiscent of some of the old trade beads, but with small glass spots on them like sea creatures, are incorporated into her jewellery. She uses the transparency of the glass to contrast with the silver links. Carol teaches in the Jewellery Department at Natal Technikon, where she works closely with the students and develops her ideas alongside theirs as she leads them through the jewellery process.

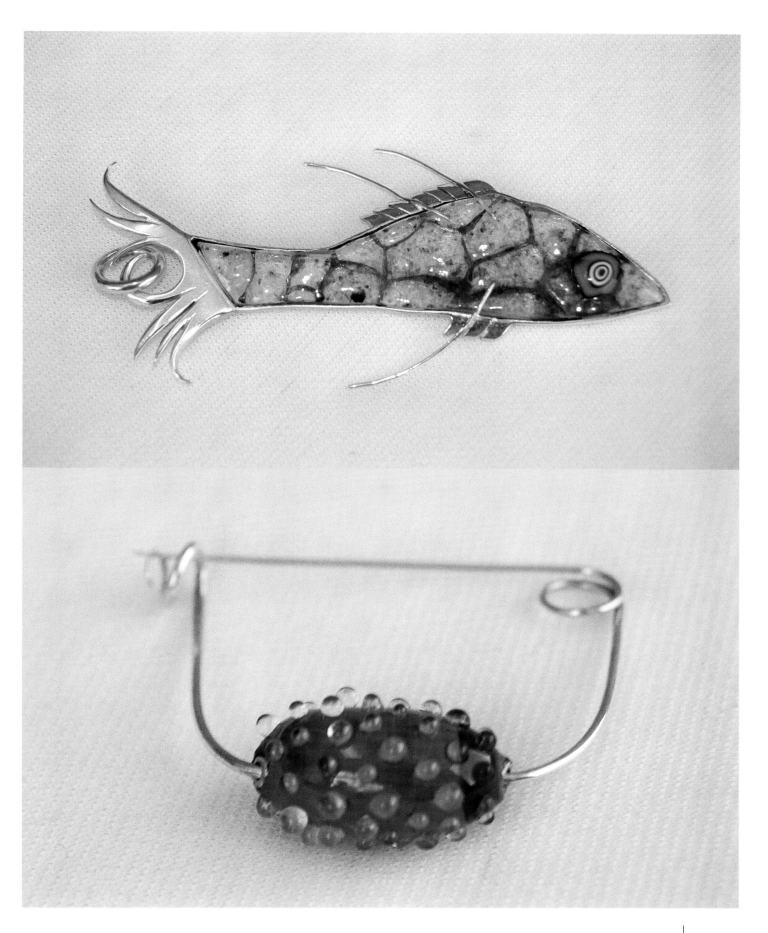

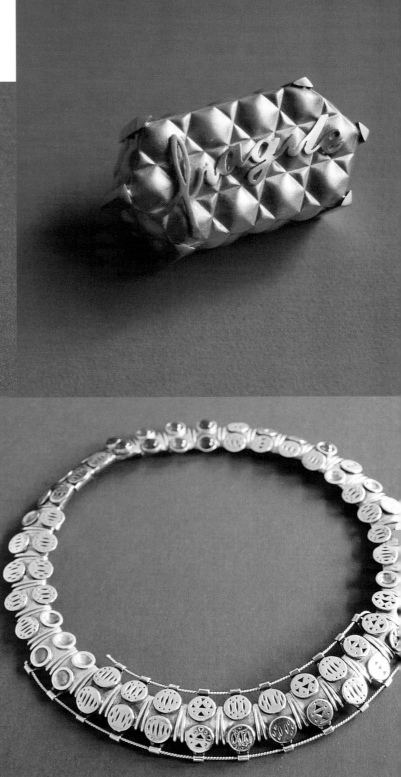

THIS PAGE, CLOCKWISE FROM LEFT:
Maritza de Beer, lecturer. Earrings. Woven silver and enamel; **Kim Boezaart**. Brooch. Gold; **Carine Terreblanche**. *Fragile*. Silver brooch; Silver Necklace designed by **Eugene Hon** and made by **William Judson**.

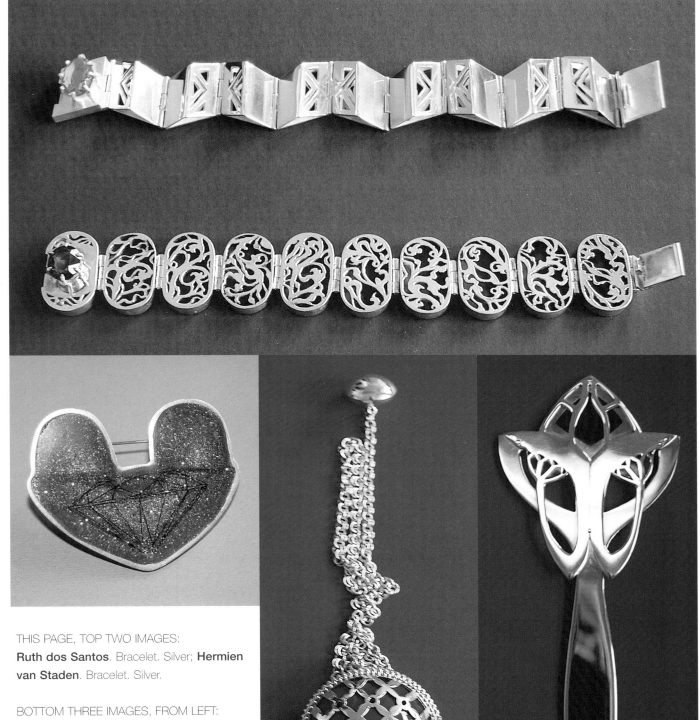

THIS PAGE, TOP TWO IMAGES:
Ruth dos Santos. Bracelet. Silver; **Hermien van Staden**. Bracelet. Silver.

BOTTOM THREE IMAGES, FROM LEFT:
Carine Terreblanche. Brooch. Silver, glitter, resin, image; **Sarah Preston**. Incense burner. Silver and enamel; **Natasha de Wet**. Letter opener. Silver, brass, perspex.

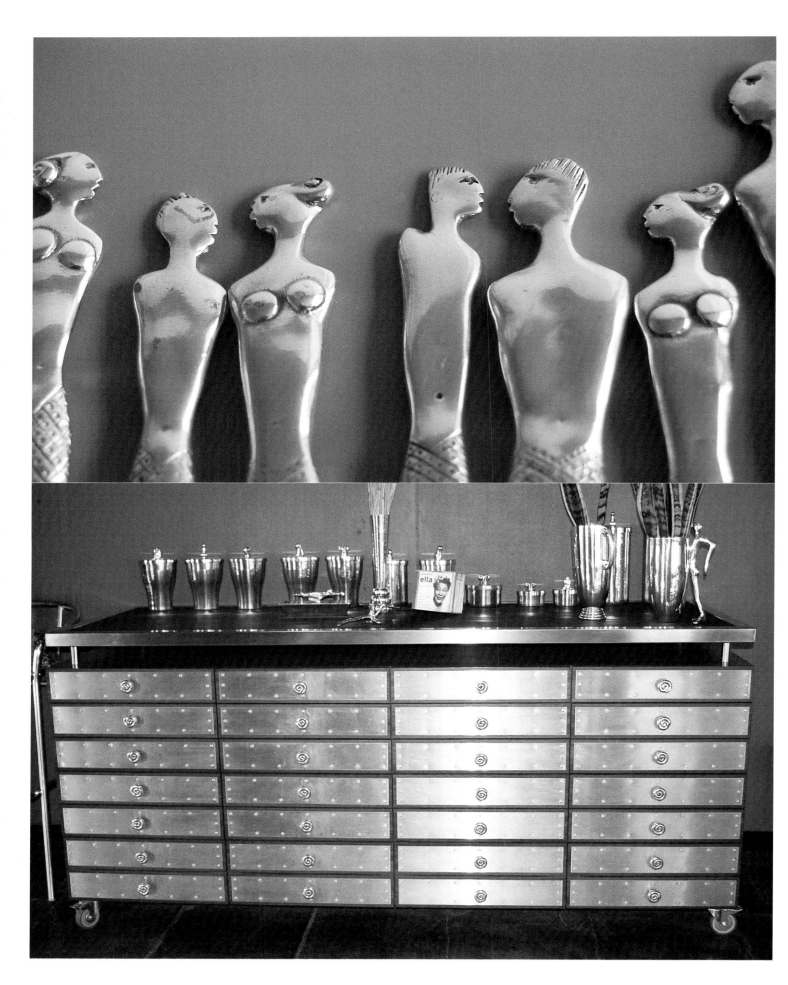

metalwork

A longside the jewellers are metalsmiths making products using the varied metals so prevalent in South Africa.

The trapeze artist hanging from the metal bar that keeps the paper napkins from flying around or the metal woman on the wall with her fingers splayed to accommodate keys are part of Carrol Boyes' product range. Fish and mermaids, figures and spirals, as well as more formalised designs, all find their way onto these products.

As you walk through the door of her Cape Town base, a wall of cast-resin comic-book images meet you and behind the service desk the wall is covered with colourful telephone-wire baskets. The handrails up the staircase were designed and handcrafted by Carrol, and the showroom is laid out with style and filled with her products. Among the fantastic array of metal objects are many charming beaded dolls from Monkey Business, a poverty-alleviation project she supports and markets. Carrol feels that the craft movement in South Africa is both innovative and exciting and that, because of all the years of isolation, local craft has developed a unique style.

Carrol Boyes manufactures cutlery, dishes and bowls, and a wide range of metal products. She has a Fine Arts degree majoring in Sculpture. After teaching for years, she set up a studio to work in copper and in pewter jewellery, but a trial teaspoon she made was almost immediately sold, so she moved on to salad servers and from there the Carrol Boyes range was launched. The range is now extensive, yet

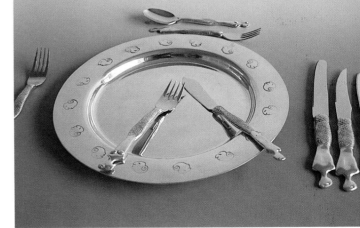

OPPOSITE PAGE, FROM TOP:
Carrol Boyes. Cutlery. Detail. Stainless steel.
Carrol Boyes. Chest of drawers with various objects from her showroom.

THIS PAGE, FROM TOP:
Carrol Boyes. Floor tile. Aluminium, pewter; **Carrol Boyes**. Dish with server and letter opener; Stainless-steel plate and cutlery.

she continues to bring her own sense of style and humour to creating the products. She says that the weekends are her time to design and plan. She gets to her spectacular apartment overlooking the Atlantic Ocean, shuts the door, turns on her music and the time is her own.

A primitive ladle used to weigh gold in the ancient markets of Africa, cut from a single piece of metal and beaten into shape, started Theresa Jo Wessels on her spoon-making career. She was intrigued by the simplicity and vigour of the design and made three spoons, which she took to the Grahamstown Festival. They were the first things to sell, so she designed other cutlery based on this concept. Theresa Jo continues to make these spoons from silver or brass, with subtle enamel work in shades of blue through to black or gold, with red copper forms inlaid into the surface of the handle. Other items of cutlery, a range of dinnerware, as well as simple jewellery, soon followed. Theresa Jo feels it is important that her work has simplicity and is not stressed – in refining the work, the spontaneity is sometimes lost.

Theresa Jo is yet another graduate of the Stellenbosch University Jewellery Design Department. She and her husband run Artvark, a shop full of her work and that of other local artists in Kalk Bay, on the Cape Peninsula.

Mirrors with broad metal frames collaged with cut-out, stylised images of people, dogs, flying objects – from birds and rockets to jumbo jets – all interspersed with palm trees and plants, household objects or images from

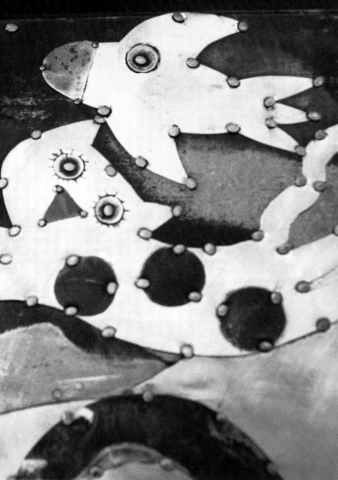

THIS PAGE, CLOCKWISE FROM TOP:
Sue Jowell. Portrait of Sue Jowell in mirror. Aluminium, brass, copper; **Sue Jowell**. Mirror. Detail; **Sue Jowell**. Key holder. Aluminium, brass, copper; **Sue Jowell**. Key holder. Detail.

THIS PAGE, FROM TOP:

Enoch Ngwenya. Wire basket. Wire and telephone wire; **Street Wires**. Radio. Mixed media including radio and wire; **Street Wires**. Bee. Wire.

OPPOSITE PAGE:

Street Wires. Baobab tree. Wire.

the sea, hang on the yellow walls of Sue Jowell's living space. The choice of image surrounds human narratives of domestic or dream topics. The brass, aluminium and copper she uses can be oxidised to give a subtle range of colours that blends or contrasts with the matte metallic surface of the frame.

After many requests from game lodges for mirrors and coat-hook panels with animals on them, she has begun a new range with all the usual game images, including a zebra with small tacks holding on the stripes. Other frames have lizards and chameleons crawling on them.

Sue studied Graphic Design at the Michaelis School of Art in Cape Town. The first frames she made were for her paintings – the mirrors came later. She feels that the fact that the mirrors are functional justifies the process of making them: 'not quite playing and not quite art'. Her humorous images are often inspired by her 'domestic chaos' caused by working at home from a small studio surrounded by the paraphernalia of two small children and a few dogs.

Metal-and-wire baobab trees, frames and many other products are made by Street Wires in Cape Town. They have a formal structure to the business of making and marketing wire products, in contrast to the many other informal groups found on almost every city street corner, making wire baskets of every form, key hooks, candelabra, plant stands, soap dishes and, in December, Christmas trees and tree decorations.

woodworking

The large wooden insects of Widus Ntshali – which could be moths or butterflies or maybe flies and mosquitoes – are carved and then their wings and legs are patterned with the popular burning technique. The dangerous-looking dogs and pigs with sharp rubber teeth made by Alpheus Ngodwane are carved, and then brightly painted and covered with spots.

Wood is used extensively by informal groups because it is a relatively inexpensive material that can be found as off-cuts at building sites or furniture factories. Rural craftspeople have an endless natural supply if they ensure that re-planting is carried out regularly. The national programme to eliminate alien vegetation has inspired the design of garden furniture, screens and objects from the large quantities of exotic saplings that are cleared. The Montebello Craft and Design Centre in Cape Town makes a range of rustic furniture, shelves and screens that are perfect for gardens and patios, while Linkie Wessels and her group in Gauteng make extra-large baskets frequently used in architectural settings and gardens.

Craftsmen working in wood are very conscious of the need to use non-indigenous woods unless they can find trees blown down in storms or the trimmings from botanical gardens. Ranges of well-crafted furniture are available all over the country and are used in coffee shops and restaurants, as well as in homes and on the veranda. The availability of boxes, bowls, spoons, cheese boards and many other household items is increasing as people return to the crafts of woodturning and carving.

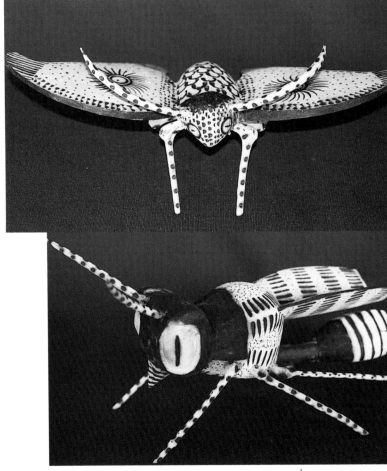

OPPOSITE PAGE:
Montebello Craft and Design Centre.
Garden furniture. Alien vegetation.

THIS PAGE, FROM TOP:
Alpheus Ngodwane. Carved wooden spotted dogs; Wood, paint and rubber; **Widus Ntshali**. Carved and burnt wooden insects.

The smooth wooden boxes made by Brian Coetzee are exquisitely constructed using different, often unusual woods as contrast. His passion for working with wood stems from the aesthetic beauty, warmth and sensuality he finds in the wood as well as its inconsistencies. He allows these opposing characteristics and qualities to dictate the size and shape of the box, but carefully selects each piece he uses with attention to colour and grain direction.

John Mills and Andrew Early are both wood turners who enjoy using the enormous variety of wood available in the country. John makes large pepper grinders using several different woods of contrasting colours. He is a conservationist and aware of the value of wood, and has now extended this conservation activity to a network of fellow craftspeople who watch for wood that may go to waste.

Andrew Early's simple, turned wooden bowls are carefully finished and polished. They are made mainly from exotic woods such as jacaranda, Indian mahogany, silky oak, pin oak and from indigenous woods when they find fallen trees in someone's garden – never from the bush.

Andrew trained as an architectural draughtsman but has now joined his father John who had been working as a wood turner for several years in the beautiful Dargle Valley of the KwaZulu-Natal Midlands.

The unusual combination of wood set in resin before turning it on a lathe has been developed by Thys Carstens from the Western Cape. The finished product shows the effect of light penetrating through the resin, sometimes subtly coloured in soft blues and greens, between the carefully chosen pieces of wood. Some of the bowls have a pattern around the periphery, while others may have the resin running across the diameter.

OPPOSITE PAGE:
Thys Carstens. Round wooden bowl. Resin and wood. (Photograph by Mark van Coller); **John Mills**. Turned wooden bowls. Curly maple and jacaranda.

THIS PAGE, FROM TOP LEFT:
Andrew Early. Turned wooden bowl; **Brian Coetzee**. Wooden box. Purple heart and yellowwood; **Schalk van Niekerk**. Turned wooden bowl. Wood, paint and rubber eye-droppers; **Schalk van Niekerk**. Turned wooden bowl. Wood and pins.

social projects

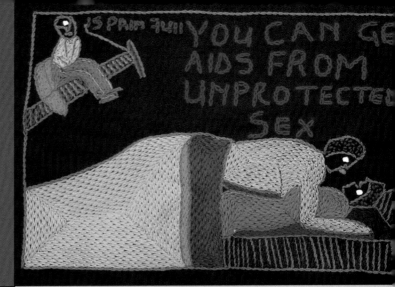

C raft has had a considerable effect on the HIV/AIDS pandemic in that it has contributed in no small way to the awareness programme, fundraising efforts, alleviation of poverty and the creation of jobs.

Many craft groups have been set up to assist people suffering from the virus as the informal structure of craft is ideal for those who need to work at their own pace and in their own time. Beautiful embroideries, beadwork and other objects are made and sold to support the families of AIDS sufferers. In addition to the financial support gained from craft, it has been found that people working together creatively are more open to educational input and discussion around their problem, its cause and what should be done to prevent infection.

Artist Proof Studio in Newtown, Johannesburg, a community-based printing studio started by Kim Berman, a master printer and lecturer in printmaking at the Technikon Witwatersrand, and Phumani Paper coordinated a national 'Paper Prayers' programme. The project intended to involve everyone – both rural and urban – in all nine provinces. The 'Paper Prayers' originates from an ancient Japanese custom of offering painted strips of paper as prayers when someone is sick. The programme has involved thousands of people in a spirit of giving and healing, and offered support to those who have HIV/AIDS. The supportive environment raises awareness of the disease and

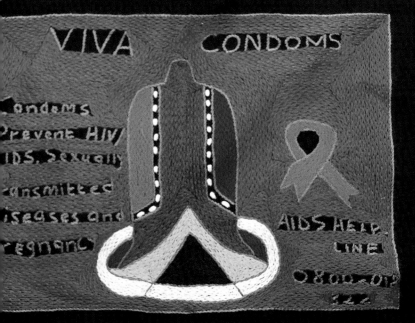

produces an artistic gesture of compassion and healing in each paper prayer. By its nature, this project involves people – to the extent that they can see their participation and contribution as part of the solution. Many of the paper prayer designs were reproduced on cloth, embroidered and combined into exceptional wall hangings and quilts.

The Kopanang Women's Embroidery Group is linked to one of the Phumani paper-making groups as well as to a care centre. The women come from Tsakane and Geluksdal, two communities that were historically divided during the apartheid era. An integral part of their being together is also to share their stories, culture and histories, and to address the HIV/AIDS issue. Kopanang means 'gathering together' and epitomises the spirit of sharing and creativity of the group.

Brightly coloured papier-mâché bowls covered in over-prints from the canning factories are made in Cape Town by Wola Nani, Xhosa for 'we embrace and develop each other'. The group was formed to help people living with HIV/AIDS to access the services they need, and to create opportunities for them to help themselves.

Women bear the brunt of the HIV/AIDS pandemic as they are historically disempowered and marginalised. They have little voice to articulate their needs or to claim the services on which their survival depends. Women can make these bowls in times of poor health as they are not

THIS PAGE AND OPPOSITE PAGE:
Kopanang Women's Embroidery Group.

labour intensive and, through the production of these highly marketable crafts, they can earn a steady and reliable income to support themselves and their dependants.

One of the most extensive AIDS programmes is the Siyazama AIDS Project – 'Striving to make a positive difference'. The project was started in 1996 as an HIV/AIDS awareness and rural crafts collaborative coordinated by Kate Wells from the School of Design at the ML Sultan Technikon in Durban.

KwaZulu-Natal has the fastest-growing AIDS epidemic in the world and it is the women and children who are most affected by the disease. Talk of love or sexual behaviour is taboo in traditional rural communities, but is perfectly acceptable through the language of beads. Expert beaded cloth doll- and tableau-makers, as well as beaded jewellery crafters, gather together to work and, simultaneously, to learn about HIV/AIDS, able to air their concerns and fears as women, as sisters, mothers and caregivers.

The workshops teach product design and innovation as well as communications and business skills, giving the women pride and an affirmation of their cultural identity and indigenous knowledge systems. At every meeting, *mphepho* – 'smoke of the ancestors' – is burnt so as to engage the good wishes of the ancestors as well as to invite their support in coping with AIDS in a positive sense. Traditional dance troupes, poets and musicians come to

THIS PAGE AND OPPOSITE PAGE:
Wola Nani. Papier-mâché bowls made around a mould using overprints from canning factories in Cape Town.

inspire the craftspeople, and information on social and health matters is discussed during the workshops.

In the early stages of the project, the red ribbon logo became the visual metaphor for transferring information and, while this is still prevalent today, the beaded cloth dolls and tableaux are now powerful art forms, portraying unique and immediate social commentary. Addressing sexually explicit issues such as 'how you get it' and questioning the escalating practice and role of 'virgin testing' in rural areas, as well the role traditional healers play in healing, has led to practical knowledge empowerment. Rural traditional craftswomen are regarded as opinion makers and have earned a degree of status within their community and, to this end, are able to provoke and promote dialogue within their homes on sensitive issues regarding the AIDS pandemic.

The workshops have made possible some of the Siyazama AIDS Project's most unusual, innovative and stirring crafts, and this growing body is a contemporary social documentary of exactly what is happening in rural areas.

OPPOSITE, FROM TOP:
Siyazama AIDS Project. Woman giving birth; Twins who have lost connection with each other as one has AIDS.

THIS PAGE, FROM TOP:
Siyazama AIDS Project. AIDS orphans. Embroidered dolls. Fabric, wire and beads; Commemorative crosses for AIDS deaths.

paper

Paper-making has become an exciting additional skill to the craft industry in the past few years. The process can be easily taught and works well as a team project, so it is a good skill to teach to poverty-alleviation groups. The many possibilities of using paper creatively for the manufacture of products or for its more traditional use for drawing, printing and painting is being extended. Individual craftspeople use paper for many products of a great variety.

Phumani Paper is a successful, innovative partnership between the government and Technikon Witwatersrand, managed and led with understanding and energy by Kim Berman. The craft of paper-making has been taught to groups in every province of the country, using either waste material such as sugarcane pulp in KwaZulu-Natal and maize stalks in the Free State or invasive aliens as used in the Western Cape. The varying materials provide a wide colour range, from soft earth tones to the olive green of invasive water plants. The quality of the paper also changes with the material and the boxes, bags and books, as well as many other products made by the groups, change from place to place.

OPPOSITE PAGE:
Handmade paper.

THIS PAGE, FROM TOP:
Liz Vels. Book. Paper, thread, paint, formed objects.
Valda Preen. Box with drawn and painted image.

THIS PAGE, FROM LEFT:
Cathy Stanley. Lights. Paper, driftwood and metal.
Verona Higgs. Bowl. Handmade paper with embossed designs on surface.

OPPOSITE PAGE, FROM TOP:
Kuyasa Products. Books, frames; **Verona Higgs** working on the surface of one of her vessels.

Kuyasa – meaning 'a new day dawning' and one of the Phumani projects based in the Western Cape – is coordinated by Cathy Stanley whose vision is to make good-quality handmade paper with dynamic, vibrant and ethnic designs. They use the pulp of the Port Jackson – an invasive alien being cleared by the Working for Water Project – to make the paper, which can be of different thicknesses, depending on its final use. Cathy's project makes cylinders and gift packs for the wine industry, as well as packaging and boxes for a paper-bead project making jewellery.

Liz Vels has been a 'compulsive maker' since she was a child. Rows of handmade books, jugs, old chairs covered with paper, poems written on every available surface, beautiful pieces of paper with seed pods, pressed flowers, leaves and cocoons imbedded into them can be found in Liz's studio. Her paper goes far beyond the craft of paper-making; in fact, she very rarely makes her own paper any more but uses the paper from Kuyasa, where her daughter Cathy Stanley is coordinator. She layers it, paints on it, writes on it,

embroiders on it, tears it and embellishes the surface in a multitude of creative ways. Her paper records her life as a mother, a lover of nature, of words, of beauty, her garden, water, flowers and colour. Liz feels that by creating beautiful things to eat off, to drink from, to walk on and to wear, craftspeople enrich our everyday lives.

The large shell-like paper vessels made by Verona Higgs both collect and reflect light. She uses the container because of its connection to the female body – as containers of memory, of life, of lost messages from the past. Valda Preen covers boxes with her drawings. She chooses suitable images to fit each box and finishes them with layers and layers of varnish until the surface is rich and glossy.

fibre

The wide range of fibre, fabric, embroidery, weaving, knitting – and all the combinations of these – is ever expanding. Fabric is designed and hand-printed all over the country in a variety of informal groups and small factories. The colour and design of a fabric can instantly change the tone of a room, and fabrics with a specific reference to Africa are no exception.

Africa Nova prints fabric by hand, using potato cuts. Margie Murgatroyd started using this process in Zimbabwe, but relocated to Cape Town, where she set up a small factory in Kommetjie. Because of the urban reference in Cape Town, the designs have changed and the patterning now includes urban houses and other familiar images, while the choice of colour is taken from the environment. Because the production is small, there can be short runs of particular colours and patterns that mutate as they go according to the design or, perhaps, the particular choice of the customers.

The craftspeople print on long tables in teams, each with a leader who marks out the cloth, and because the print becomes less and less distinct, they cut new designs on the halved potatoes each day.

Margie feels that South African craft has been stimulated by the market place and is now acquiring a national identity. There is a strong cross link between European and African backgrounds using Western technology with traditional craft and vice versa, but there is always a need for references to maintain the originality. The Philani Flagship Printing Project, producing brightly printed,

OPPOSITE PAGE:
Africa Nova. Fabric designs printed with potato cuts.

THIS PAGE, FROM TOP:
Philani Flagship Printing Project. Fabric. Detail;
Africa Nova potato cut showing design for printing;
Philani Flagship Printing Project. Fabric. Detail.

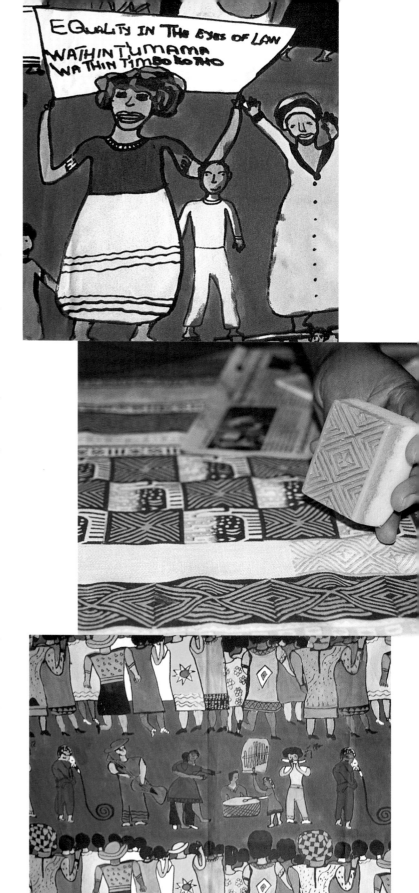

hand-coloured cloths depicting everyday township life and happenings, or household images of tea, Coca-Cola or familiar brands of cereal printed on large cloths and cushion covers, is an example of this linkage. Sometimes, images with a sociopolitical theme, such as AIDS or women's rights, are also produced.

Many creative craftspeople, using a variety of materials and techniques in their work, are 'compulsive makers' who have gathered skills throughout their working life and use them to make objects or installations, often for their own use and enjoyment, but sometimes commercially.

Both Penny Cornell and Celia de Villiers work predominantly in textiles and thread. Penny finds her inspiration in an inescapable love of colour and texture and, in her desire to combine the two, has chosen stitchery, thread and fabric as her media. She is excited by heaps of threads and piles of beads, 'turned on' by a selection of vibrant silk and metallic fabrics. She currently works in Cape Town, designing and stitching exclusive items, such as beaded amulet purses, embroidered purses and bags, and larger works for exhibition and commission, using beadwork, canvas work, appliqué and machine embroidery techniques. She hand-dyes thread and fabrics for use in her own work and for sale. Penny studied art, design and embroidery in London and still continues her studies in Embroidery and Creative Studies.

Celia de Villiers embroiders by hand and machine and weaves together other materials such as wood and wire. The resulting rich surface textures are dyed using various natural and chemical substances so as to create fibre sculptures. Recently, she has been researching signs, symbols and beliefs connected to adornment of the body. Celia also works in glass, making softly formed boxes and containers.

Jutta Faulds uses handmade felt in many of her hangings and ceremonial garments, together with fabrics of all kinds – feathers and now metal, ceramics and paper and whatever other materials she feels the piece needs. Her house is filled with fabrics, threads of all colours, beads, buttons and sequins and a myriad other materials packed into old haberdashery shop chests of drawers. She puts enormous energy into teaching adults to use their skills to make objects of self-expression.

Carla Wasserthal is a lecturer in the Department of Textile Design and Technology at the Pretoria Technikon, where she has set students on the path to become self-sufficient within the creative genre; her philosophy is that art and teaching is a multifaceted preparation for the art of living, a continuous creative dilemma.

Carla has a formal Textile Design qualification and her own work incorporates layers of textiles – mostly recycled – that are cut, folded, tinted and dyed. At present she makes cloth bowls, chairs, baskets and garments but will always migrate to new creative ideas as they arise. Carla also assists her husband in his candle-making business and craft and design shop in Pretoria.

OPPOSITE, CLOCKWISE FROM BOTTOM:
Penny Cornell. Amulet and purse. Beads, canvas, hand-dyed threads; **Celia de Villiers**. 'Lobola 2000' (part of ritual garment series). Handcrafted felt, textiles, hand-knitting, cotton rope, perspex, handcrafted glass, cowrie shells, machine embroidery, hand quilted.

THIS PAGE, FROM LEFT:
Carla Wasserthal. Bowl. *Revised Exodus*. Discarded linen and cotton, jute, plant material, rust, carbon pigment, wire, fungi-free polycell; **Jutta Faulds**. Detail. Sunbird. Fabric, metal.

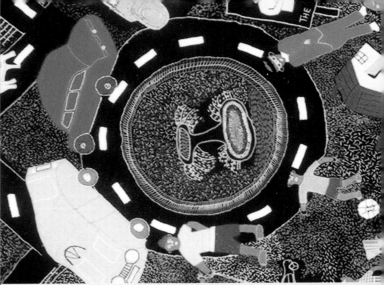

mpumalanga cloth

The cloth made for the Legislative Assembly Chamber at the Riverside Government Complex in Nelspruit was coordinated by the Mpumalanga Department of Sports, Arts, Recreation and Culture in 1999.

The process of commissioning the biggest public artwork to be designed and made by rural women in South Africa began late in 1998. The final piece was 35 metres long and 3.2 metres high, the black cloth background worked with beads, wire, embroidery threads and fabric pieces.

Women from two areas were chosen to make the wall hanging: a group of Ndebele beadworkers from Kwaggafontein – coordinated by Anna Mahlangu, the wife of the local chief, who for many years had been running a beadwork cooperative – and a smaller group from Ekulendeni near the Swazi border. There were 56 craftspeople in total.

Twelve designers were selected from the group after they had all done a series of drawing exercises. The beaders examined new ways of putting their beadwork expertise to work while the others were instructed in a variety of embroidery stitches and appliqué techniques.

Meanwhile, the Department of Sports, Arts, Recreation and Culture put together a panel of experts to assemble the history and stories that should be reflected in the artwork. These were sourced from books, including previously banned Umkhonto we Sizwe publications, and old photographs, such as those depicting metalsmiths at work in the 1880s, and even the ballot sheet from the country's first democratic election in 1994.

The designers spent an intensive two weeks working together from the original images. The brief was to tell the entire story of Mpumalanga, from the first signs of life to the events of the 1990s. Although the panel is huge, many fascinating events and images had to be left out. It was decided that a red thread would unite the diversity of the piece. This starts out as blood from the nose of the rain bull (a rock art reference) and develops into footpaths, then dirt tracks, a railway line and finally the Maputo Corridor. The main theme of the work is the trade routes that connect the ancient past of Mpumalanga to the economy of today.

At the entrance to the Legislative Assembly Chamber one is greeted by the self-portraits and names of the women who worked on the panel. The portraits are done in a combination of beadwork, appliqué and embroidery. Some of the women are in traditional dress and others in shiny gold earrings and braided hairstyles. It is quite moving to walk past these 'silent' women before one enters the most important room for the democratic government in the province, where the panel is hung on the wall of the circular chamber. The importance of this panel cannot be underestimated. In its essence, it represents the new South Africa.

THIS PAGE AND OPPOSITE PAGE:
Mpumalanga Cloth. Mpumalanga Legislature Assembly Chamber, Nelspruit.

weaving

Traditional craft techniques from other countries have, on occasion, been assimilated into local crafts and the boundaries have now become blurred. Weaving is one of the techniques that was brought from Scandinavia and Britain and other parts of Africa where it was well developed. Today, there are rug, tapestry and cloth weavers as well as spinners and dyers using local cotton, wool, mohair and mopane silk.

Many of the rug designs at The Weavers' Hut are taken from Zulu references and woven in warm earth tones and often in black, white and tan. They were initially woven using cotton knit strips, but now pure wool is used and they can be produced in any size. Eleanor McCarthy started the project 15 years ago in Donnybrook, a rural area of the KwaZulu-Natal Midlands, to provide job opportunities for women in the area. Natal Weavers is also in this area, but weaves cotton into brightly striped fabrics that are made into colourful bags, cushion covers and hammocks.

Botshabelo Weavers is situated in the Free State. They create weavings and tapestries in pure mohair, depicting scenes of Basotho homesteads and rural landscapes.

Saskia Williams is a fibre artist who uses the loom to make large woven hangings, usually for commissions for both private homes and the foyers of office buildings and public spaces. For her, it is the colour, together with the tactile and textural quality of the weaving, that is important in the finished piece.

OPPOSITE PAGE:
Natal Weavers. Woven, brightly coloured fabrics.

THIS PAGE:
Natal Weavers. Woven, brightly coloured hammock.
Detail; **Weaver's Hut**. Pure wool woven carpet.

conclusion

The excitement and ongoing creativity generated throughout the country is reaching a maturity that is making its mark on world craft. There are constant requests for exhibitions in many major cities overseas, which will serve to remind international buyers and collectors that South Africa is a craft-making country of note.

Knowledge of the old will always remain as the skills and techniques are being studied and recorded by academic institutions and there are still people who remember the techniques of their grandparents and are of aware of their importance. Transitional and contemporary craft must be nurtured and developed, but neither should take precedence over the other. New techniques and processes are constantly being explored and new products designed. With the diversity of cultures and concepts abounding, there will always be a wealth of creativity in the country.

OPPOSITE PAGE:
Jacques Coetzer. Figure. **Ardmore**. Candleholder. Ceramic. (Photograph by David Ross)

THIS PAGE, FROM TOP LEFT:
Ania Krajewska. *Image bagging*. Aluminium, perspex, computer prints, parachute fabric; Xhosa bag; **Carla Wasserthal**. Wire bag

index

OPPOSITE PAGE:
Victor Mpopo. Ceramic figures. Mandela and Graca.

acknowledgements

Craft South Africa – Traditional Transitional Contemporary was made possible through the interest and collaboration of a great many people.

Firstly, we would like to thank Phillip Stein for having the vision of a book of South African craft, which is now a reality. We would like to thank Dusanka Stojakovic of Pan Macmillan, South Africa, for her determination to publish a book on South African craft having seen the FNB Vita Craft Awards Exhibition in 2000. Thanks, too, to the publishing team: Louise Grantham of the-e-junction and Zann Hoad of Sharp Sharp Media, who guided us through the process of publishing the book and to Pat Tucker and then Sean Fraser of PHRASEworks for editing the text.

First National Bank offered generous support for the book and has sponsored the FNB Vita Craft Awards Exhibitions for the past nine years. We thank them very sincerely for this ongoing belief in crafts and its potential to grow into a means of support for many South Africans.
The creative contribution of the book designer, Lore Watterson, and her team at DeskLink Publishing made it possible to combine the text and the pictures into a fine book – which is exactly as we wanted it to look. Thanks to Megan Larter and Sappi Fine Paper for their enthusiasm and generous support of the project.

We are also grateful to the many colleagues who spent time and care in the preparation of the expert inserts in each chapter:
- Thomas N. Huffman, Professor of Archaeology, University of the Witwatersrand – 'Archaeology Background'
- Muffin Stevens, Senior Lecturer, Pretoria Technikon – 'Philosophy of Crafts'
- Meleleke Frank Ledimo, Senior Curator, University of Witwatersrand Art Galleries – 'The Heritage of Craft'
- Dr Rayda Becker, Curator, Art Work, Parliament – 'Exhibitions and Craft'
- Jannetje van der Merwe (Department Corporate Communications and Marketing, UNISA) and Professor Brenda Schmahmann (Head, Department of Fine Art, Rhodes University) for information on the Mapula Project and Karosswerkers
- Fiona Rankin-Smith and Julia Charlton, Curators, University of the Witwatersrand Art Galleries – 'Beadwork'
- Chris de Beer, Head, Jewellery Department, Natal Technikon – 'Transitional Jewellery'
- Tamar Mason and Marisa Fick-Jordaan – 'Product Development'
- Clementina van der Walt – 'The Production Path'
- Kate Wells, Lecturer, School of Design, ML Sultan Technikon, Durban – 'Siyazama Aids Project'

Many friends and colleagues in the craft industry who run galleries and shops kindly lent us their stock to photograph or gave us free range to photograph whatever we needed:
- Art Africa, Johannesburg – Carin Milling and Linda Malcolm
- Kim Sacks Gallery, Johannesburg – Kim Sacks
- Piece at the Saxon Hotel, Johannesburg – Eugenie Drake
- Zwashu Gallery, near Thohayandou, Limpopo – Alice Netshidzivhani
- Pietersburg Gallery (The Irish House) – Polokwane, Limpopo
- Bayside Gallery, Durban – Sue Greenberg
- The BAT Shop, Durban – Marisa Fick-Jordaan
- African Art Centre, Durban – Anthea Martin
- Montebello Design Centre, Cape Town – Tessa Graaff
- Kamatoka, Cape Town – Cheryl Rumbak
- Eshowe Museum & Vukani Craft Shop, Eshowe
- Heartworks, Cape Town – Margaret Woermann
- Clementina Ceramics & Fine Art, Cape Town – Clementina van der Walt

The curators of a number of museums allowed us to photograph their invaluable collections:
- SASOL African Heritage Exhibition, University of Pretoria, Mapungubwe Exhibition – Sian Tiley
- National Cultural History Museum, Pretoria, for the Schroda figurines – Johnny van Schalkwyk and Niel Muller
- Standard Bank African Art Collection, University of the Witwatersrand Art Galleries – Rayda Becker, Fiona Rankin-Smith, Julia Charlton, Amos Letsoalo

Teaching Institutions showed enormous interest in this volume:
- Jewellery Department, Stellenbosch University – Errico Cassar and Ronel Steyn
- Jewellery Department, Technikon of the Witwatersrand – Melitza de Beer
- Jewellery Department, Natal Technikon, Durban – Chris de Beer
- ML Sultan Technikon, Durban – Kate Wells
- Artist Proof Studios, Newtown, Johannesburg – Kim Berman

Our thanks, too, to Mark van Coller, Cape Town, who took a number of photographs, which unfortunately had to be reshot after the courier service vehicle was hijacked.
Friends, colleagues and associates also allowed us into their homes, offices and hotels to photograph objects in their space. This was a very important aspect of the book and we are very grateful for their kind cooperation:
- Ken and Jean Purser – USA
- Eugene Hon – Technikon of the Witwatersrand, Johannesburg
- Faan and Lucia Burger – Johannesburg
- John and Wilma Cruise – Johannesburg
- Kim Sacks – Johannesburg
- Karel Nel – Johannesburg
- Max and Audrey Coleman – Johannesburg
- Marlene and Keith Hollis – Johannesburg
- Susan and Robert Benvenuti – Johannesburg
- Sam and Peggy van Coller – Cape Town
- Helen de Leeuw – Cape Town
- Noria Mabasa – Venda
- Carrol Boyes – Cape Town
- Jane Bedford – Durban
- Mdukatshani Project, KwaZulu-Natal – Creina Alcock and Natty Duma
- Kangra Group (Pty) Ltd – Johannesburg
- Webber Wentzel Bowens – Johannesburg
- Sandton Conference Centre – Johannesburg
- Wilson & Associates (interiors: Airport Sun Intercontinental, Johannesburg)
- David Muirhead for his interior styling support and Frances Janisch – 091 9172021694 (photography: Airport Sun Intercontinental, Johannesburg)
- Saxon Hotel – Hyde Park, Johannesburg
- Western Cape Hotel & Spa – Arabella Country Estate, Western Cape

We met many craftspeople and talked to them either about their methods and techniques or their concept of crafts in general. They appear in the text, but we would like to thank them all for their information and endless patience.
Finally, we would also like to thank our families for allowing us the time and space to complete this book.

THIS PAGE, FROM TOP:
Richtersveld Arts and Craft. Ceramic planter with indigenous plant; **Candice Fenianos**. Ceramic bowl; **Hylton Nel**. Hump moulded plate.

bibliography

BOOK REFERENCES

Dormer, P. (Ed.) 1997. *The Culture of Craft – Status and Future*. Manchester: Manchester University Press; Chapter 2 'The History of Craft' – Paul Greenhalgh; Chapter 4 'Craft and Art, Culture and Biology' – Bruce Metcalf.

Williamson, Sue. 1989. *Resistance Art in South Africa*. Cape Town: David Philip Publishers. London: Catholic Institute for International Relations.

Younge, G. 1988. *Art of the South African Township*. London: Thames & Hudson.

EXHIBITION CATALOGUE REFERENCES

Emhlabeni – From the Earth. 10 June – 24 July 1993. The Standard Bank Gallery. An exhibition of traditional vessels and contemporary clay works from the Standard Bank Collection of African Art, permanenetly housed at the University Art Galleries, University of the Witwatersrand, Johannesburg. Curated by Fiona Rankin-Smith, assisted by Karel Nel and Joanne Glazer. Brochure prepared by Fiona Rankin-Smith, Karel Nel and Rayda Becker.

Evocations of the Child – Fertility Figures of the Southern African Region. 1998. Johannesburg Art Gallery. Curated by Karel Nel and Nesser Liebhammer. Cape Town: Human & Rousseau (Pty) Ltd.

The Neglected Tradition – Towards a New History of South African Art (1930–1988). 23 November 1988 – 8 January 1989. Johannesburg Art Gallery. Guest Curator: Steven Sack.

Listen to Africa. 12–14 September 2001. Chicago USA. Marissa Fick-Jordaan – General Manager: The BAT Shop, Pat Johnson – Conference Convenor.

National Craft Imbizo Showcase. October 2001. Printing College, Johannesburg. Curated by Susan Sellschop and Jerry Mabuza. Selected by Connie Chiume, Sibongile Nene, Wendy Goldblatt, Frieda le Grange. Administered by Eunice Mothetho.

Clothing and Identity – Soccer is Power! Popular Culture in South Africa March 1997–December 2001. University of the Witwatersrand Art Galleries. Curated by Fiona Rankin-Smith.

JOURNALS AND NEWS ARTICLES

Artist Proof Studio. Information Brochure 2001. Kim Berman – Programme Manager. Cara Walters – Studio Manager.

Report on the Hand Papermaking Poverty Relief Programme. July 2001. Kim Berman – Programme Manager.

McIntyre, Kate. 'Harmony in Space'. *Crafts*. No 173 Nov/Dec 2001. London: Crafts Council (British), 44a Pentonville Rd., London NI 9BY.

Cultural Industries Growth Strategy Summary 2000. Department of Arts, Culture, Science and Technology.

Wright, Emma. 'Story of an African Farmhouse'. *House and Leisure*. No 100. March 2002.

Msomi, S'thembiso. 'People — Craft Work'. *Sunday Times Lifestyle*. 12 November 2000.

Isaacson, Maureen. 'Karel Nel Curates Show of 15th-Century Art'. *Sunday Times*. April 2002.

OPPOSITE PAGE:

Saskia Williams. *Divided Spectrum*. Handwoven wall panel. (Collection: Kangra Group (Pty) Ltd.)

THIS PAGE:

Wire-and-bead insects.

REFERENCES FOR *The Archaeological Background*

By Tom Huffman. School of Geography, Archaeology and Environmental Studies, University of the Witwatersrand.

Aquina, M. 1968. 'Mutimwi – A Note on the Waist Belt of the Karanga'. *NADA* 9 (5), 3-4.

Aschwanden, H. 1982. *Symbols of Life*. Gweru: Mambo Press.

Berglund, A-I. 1976. *Zulu Thought – Patterns and Symbolism*. Cape Town: David Philip Publishers.

Evers, T.M. 1988. 'The Recognition of Groups in the Iron Age of Southern Africa'. (PhD Thesis). Johannesburg: University of Witwatersrand.

Fouché, L. 1937. *Mapungubwe – Ancient Bantu Civilization on the Limpopo*. Cambridge: Cambridge University Press.

Freeman-Grenville, G.S.P. 1962. *The East African Coast – Selected Documents from the First to the Earlier Nineteenth Centuries*. Oxford: Clairborne Publishers.

Gardner, G.A. 1963. *Mapungubwe – Volume II*. Pretoria: J.L. van Schaik.

Goodall, E. 1960. 'A Specific and Early Pottery Tradition of Northern Mashonaland'. *Proceedings of the First Federal Science Congress*, 441–451. Salisbury, Rhodesia.

Greenburg, J.H. 1955. *Studies in African Linguistic Classification*. New Haven: Yale University Press.

Hanisch, E.O.M. 1980. 'Interpretation of Certain Iron Age Sites in the Limpopo/Shashi Valley'. (Masters Dissertation). Pretoria: University of Pretoria.

Herbert, E. 1983. *Iron, Gender and Power – Rituals of Transformation in African Societies*. Bloomington: Indiana University Press.

Herbert, E. 1984. *Red Gold of Africa – Copper in Pre-colonial History and Culture*. Madison: University of Wisconsin Press.

Huffman, T.N. 1976. 'Gokomere Pottery from the Tunnel Site, Gokomere Mission'. *South African Archaeological Bulletin* 31, pp. 31–53.

Huffman, T.N. 1996. *Snakes and Crocodiles – Power and Symbolism in Ancient Zimbabwe*. Johannesburg: Witwatersrand University Press.

Inskeep, R.R., and Maggs, T.M. 1975. 'Unique Art Objects in the Iron Age of the Transvaal'. *South African Archaeological Bulletin* 30, pp. 114–38.

Maggs, T.M., and Davidson, P. 1981. 'The Lydenburg Heads and the Earliest African Sculpture South of the Equator'. African Arts 14 (2), pp. 28–33.

Mason, R.J. 1986. 'Origins of Black People of Johannesburg and the Southern Western Central Transvaal AD350–1880'. (Occasional Paper 16). Johannesburg: University of the Witwatersrand Archaeological Research Unit.

Matenga, E. 1993. 'Archaeological Figurines from Zimbabwe'. *Studies in African Archaeology* 5. Uppsala: Societas Archaeologica Upzaliensis.

Mayr, F. 1906. 'The Zulu Kafirs of Natal'. *Anthropos* 1, pp. 453–72.

Nettleton, A.C.E. 1984. 'The Traditional Woodcarving of the Venda and Shona'. (PhD Thesis). Johannesburg: University of the Witwatersrand.

Robinson, K.R. 1959. *Khami Ruins*. Cambridge: Cambridge University Press.

Roumeguere, P., and Roumeguere-Eberhardt, J. 1960. 'Poupées de Fertilité et Figurines d'Argile'. *Journal de la Société des Africanistes* 30, pp. 205–23.

Summers, R. 1957. 'Human Figurines in Clay and Stone from Southern Rhodesia and Adjoining Territories'. (Occasional Paper). National Museums of Southern Rhodesia 21A, pp. 61–75.

Theal, G.M. 1898–1903. *Records of South-Eastern Africa*. (Volume I). London: Government of the Cape Colony.

Vansina, J. 1984. 'Western Bantu Expansion'. *Journal of African History* 25, pp. 129–46.

Vogel, C.A.M. 1985. 'The Traditional Mural Art of the Pedi of Sekhukhuneland'. (Masters Dissertation). Johannesburg: University of the Witwatersrand.

Wood, M. 2000. 'Making Connections – Relationships between International Trade and Glass Beads from the Shashe-Limpopo Area. *South African Archaeological Society Goodwin Series* 8, pp. 78–90.

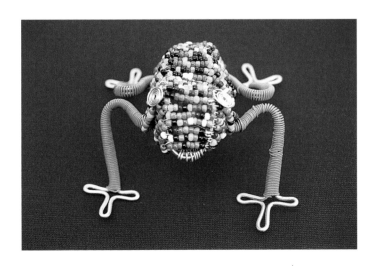

galleries and museums
galleries and museums

GAUTENG
Johannesburg

ART AFRICA
52 Tyrone Avenue
Parkview
011-486-2052
artafrica@yebo.co.za

BRiGHT HOUSE
Cnr 9th Street
Mellville
011-726-5657
brighthouse@yebo.co.za

GERTRUDE POSEL GALLERY
Wits University Galleries
Senate House
Jorissen Street
Braamfontein
011-717-3632
gallery@atlas.wits.ac.za

LINDAFRIKA
Shop 6, Reithmere
Cnr Corlett & Delta Roads
Birnam
011-887-7814
lindafrika@freemail.apsa.co.za

JOHANNESBURG ART GALLERY
Joubert Park
Klein Street, City
011-725-3130
art@mj.org.za

KIM SACKS GALLERY
153 Jan Smuts Avenue
Parkwood
011-447-5804
kim@kimsacksgallery.com

MUKONDENI AFRICAN ART GALL.
36 Orleans Road
Inanda, Kya Sands
011-708-2116
africanart@mukondeni.com

MUSEUMAFRICA
121 Bree Street,
Newtown Cultural Precinct
011-833-5624
museumafrica@jhb.org.za

PIECE
Saxon Hotel
Saxon Road, Sandhurst
011-292-6000
info@piece.co.za

GAUTENG
Pretoria

AFRICA WINDOW MUSEUM
Cnr Bosman & Visagie Streets
Pretoria
012-324-6082

ASSOCIATION OF ARTS
173 Mackie Street
New Muckleneuk
012-346-3100
artspta@mweb.co.za

KLAUS WASSERTHAL
88 Cilliers Street
Sunnyside
012-344-5797

MILLENNIUM GALLERY
75 George Storrer Avenue
Groenkloof
012-460-8217
mgallery@mweb.co.za

KWAZULU-NATAL
Durban

AFRICAN ART CENTRE
P.O. BOX 603
Durban
031-304-7915
afriart1@iafrica.com

THE BAT SHOP
The BAT Centre
45 Maritime Place
Small Craft Harbour, Esplanade
031-332-9951
batcraft@mineb.co.za

BAYSIDE GALLERY
The BAT Centre
45 Maritime Place
Small Craft Harbour,
Esplanade
031-368-5547

TECHNIKON NATAL ART GALLERY
Berea Campus
Natal Technikon
Durban
031-204-2207

WESTERN CAPE
Cape Town

ARTVARK
48 Main Road
Kalk Bay
021-788-5584
artvark@iafrica.com

AFRICA NOVA
Main Road
Hout Bay
021-790-4454
canova@iafrica.com

CLEMENTINA'S CERAMICS &
FINE ART
31 Breda Street
Oranjezicht
021-421-2025
clement@netactive.co.za

HEARTWORKS
98 Kloof Street
Gardens
021-424-8419

PETER VISSER GALLERY
117 Long Street
Cape Town
021-423-7870

PETER VISSER GIFTS
63 Loop Street
Cape Town
021-422-2660

S.A. NATIONAL GALLERY
Government Avenue
Cape Town
021-467-4660

THE KIRSTENBOSCH SHOP
Rhodes Drive
Newlands
021-762-2510

MONTEBELLO
31 Newlands Road
Newlands
021-685-6445
montebello@telkomsa.net

THE POTTER'S SHOP
6 Rouxville Road
Kalk Bay
021-788-7030
silverstone@gem.co.za